# The Little Book of Big Emotions

A simple guide to understanding and
managing emotion

BY PHIL SLADE

Published by INHOUSE PUBLISHING™ 2026

Third Editions. First edition Published by Decida Digital Publishing, 2025



For all feedback and correspondence email support@switch4schools.com.au

ISBN  978-1-923746-14-5

To learn more about Switch4Schools visit

www.switch4schools.com

# Contents

*"If it's mentionable,*

*it's manageable"*

- Fred Rodgers

# Let's Start At The Very Beginning

*It's a very good place to start!*

Emotions. They help us survive in a chaotic world, but they can also make life much more complicated than it needs to be. This little book is all about better understanding and managing emotions so we can live more peaceful, meaningful, successful lives.

So what are emotions?

*Well, there is a clue in the word itself...*
*[e][motion]*

[Motion] comes from the Latin "motere", which means 'to move' or 'energy in motion'. Roman troops used motere to discuss troop movements. [E] simply implies that motion is away from something. Today we think of e-motions as feelings that move you away or toward something. Emotions fuel action.

# [e][motion]

| Latin prefix "**e—**" or "**ex—**" "out of, from" | latin root: **motere** "to move" |
|---|---|
| | *noun* |
| *connotes "move away" (think ex-it)* | the action or process of moving or being moved |

In around 1579, French academics evolved the word 'motere' into **émouvoir,** which was a catch-all phrase to talk about our internal energy states, passion, sentiments and affections (to move, to stir up, to affect, to disturb or to arouse). For the first time in human history scientists had a way to think about and examine what was going on inside us.

### Dieu merci pour le français passionné!
*(Translation: Thank goodness for the passionate French!)*

This concept didn't emerge in the less passionate English language as 'emotion' until the 1830's - which wasn't all that long ago, so it's not surprising that we're still trying to figure it all out!

It was 250 years between the word emotion emerging in French and English.

# So, Why Do We Have Emotions?

*Wouldn't life be easier without them?*

Emotions are actually designed to help us. They are like **our very own superpowers** that have helped us become the most dominant species on the planet. They help us identify danger, leap to action, give us energy, attract us to others, and help us work together. They are not good or bad, they just are.

The better we can understand and manage these emotion superpowers, the better we will be!

The first step in mastering the superpower of emotions is to be able to label them. Our brain needs words in order to think about things, so let's have a look at how we can do this usir Switch Emotion Wheel™.

# Emotions = *information + fuel for action*

# The Switch Emotion Wheel™®

*A nice way to map out and understand emotions.*

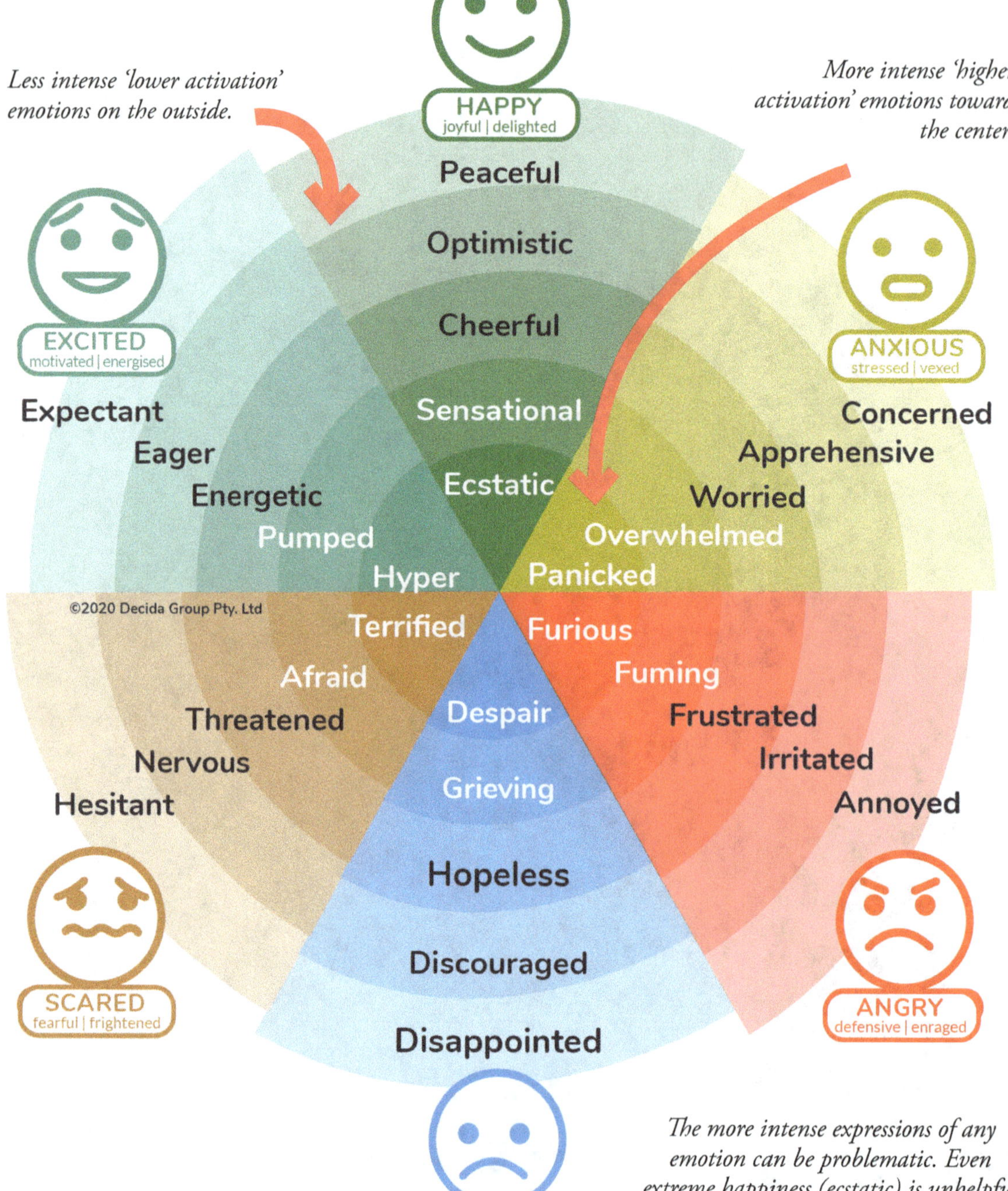

The Switch Emotion Wheel™ is helpful, because our brain needs words and language to be able to think about anything. Try thinking about something now that you don't have a word for... It's pretty much impossible! Words are conceptual vessels that allow us to think.

Saying you're **furious** is one thing, but knowing that it is the most extreme form of anger helps us think about fury in a new way. Language and intensity levels work together to become a conceptual framework that allows us to better understand and manage emotion.

When we don't want to get dragged into a full emotional conversation, we tend to default to the classic lines:

### "I'm fine." Or "Good".

Which usually means one of two things. "I've got this under control, don't worry about it." Or, "I have no idea how I'm feeling, and I really don't want to think about it right now."

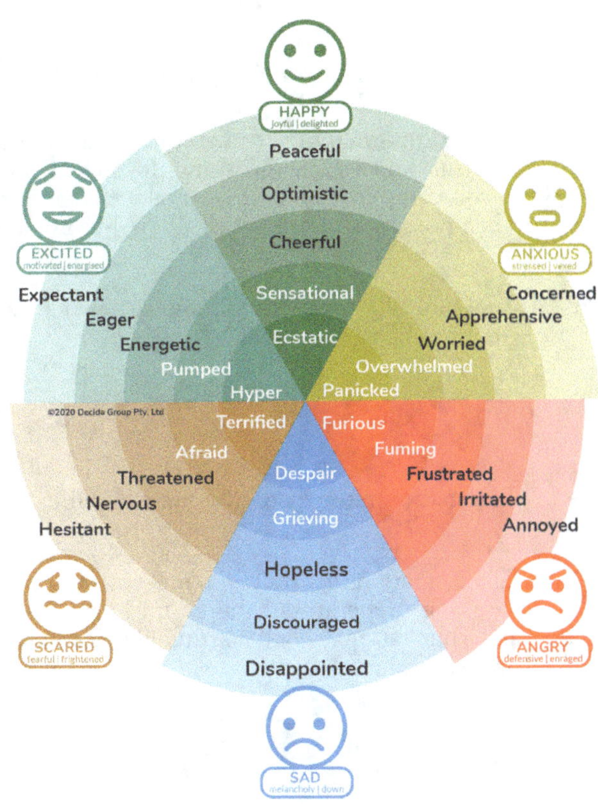


That's not laziness. It's learnt.

Most only know haow to use very basic emotion words: happy, sad, angry, anxious, scared, excited. They're helpful, but they're also pretty vague. The problem is, when you say something like "I'm angry," people don't know if you mean slightly annoyed or absolutely furious. So they start asking questions. Lots of questions. Which is exactly what you were trying to avoid.

So if you want to explain how you feel without turning it into a whole thing, or understand better what's going on inside for yourself, the trick is to be a bit more specific. Not more dramatic. Just clearer.

Instead of saying, "I'm angry about that," try, "I'm a bit annoyed that decision seems unfair" Same idea. Much easier for the other person to understand. "Annoyed" sounds a lot calmer than "angry," and adding a bit of context means they don't have to guess what you mean. And when people don't have to guess, they're less likely to overreact or dig deeper than you want.

So the goal isn't to say more.

It's to say it better.

# Dialling It Up and Down

*choosing the right intensity for the right context*

It's also important to note that somewhere in the third level of each emotion (hopeless, irritated, cheerful, worried, energetic and threatened) we seem to lose control of our emotions, and our unconscious emotional drivers take charge of our thoughts and actions. This can be helpful when needing to escape from a lion, but not as useful or helpful in everyday modern life.

Another really useful thing about the Switch Emotion Wheel™ is that it helps you think about emotions like a volume dial.

### *Not just "what am I feeling?" But "how strong is it?"*

That matters more than most people realise.

When emotions get really intense, your thinking brain basically goes offline. You're not calmly weighing things up anymore. You're on autopilot. Your emotional system has taken over, and your rational brain has quietly stepped out for a moment. That's why things can feel overwhelming so quickly.

*This end of the scale is where our emotions are out of our control.*

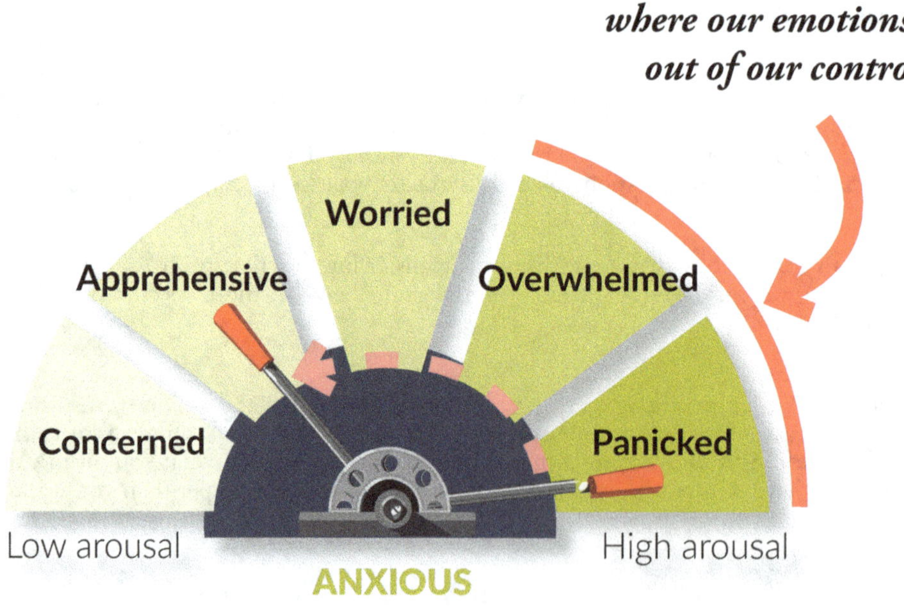

But here's the useful part.

*If you can recognise that intensity, you can start to dial it back.*

For example, instead of going from "I'm panicking" and staying there, you might shift it to "I'm feeling a bit nervous" or "I'm a bit unsure." You're not pretending the feeling isn't there. You're just turning the volume down to a level you can actually manage. That small shift helps you stay in control.

It works with other people too. If someone is really worked up (say they're feeling overwhelmed or panicked), matching that level of intensity doesn't help. It just turns the volume up even more. Instead, you meet them in the same emotion family, but at a lower level.

So if they're anxious, you might respond with concern rather than panic. "I can see why that's worrying," instead of jumping in at full intensity with them. What tends to happen is they start to feel understood, which makes them feel safer… and when people feel safe, their emotional intensity naturally comes down.

Panic dials down to concern. Concern becomes focus. That's the goal.

The real skill here is figuring out two things:
- What emotion they're actually feeling, and
- What it's about.

And those two aren't always as obvious as they seem at first.

This is what real empathy looks like. Understanding and clearly articulating another persons emotion, and what it is they are emotional about, to help them feel heard and bring the intensity down, rather than accidentally turning it up.

HAPPY
Peaceful
Cheerful
Ecstatic
EXCITED
Expectant
Energetic
Hyperactive
Overwhelmed
ANXIOUS
Concerned
Worried
Terrified
Furious
Threatened
Frustrated
Despair
Hesitant
Annoyed
ANGRY
Hopeless
SCARED
Disappointed
SAD

# The different levels of Emotion Wheels

*Four wheels to match different levels of familiarity and maturity*

## Level One (foundation)

We all have to start somewhere. Level one is best suited for those who are only just learning to use emotional words. This can be people of any age (4 tends to be a good starting point) who are simply trying to identify the things inside them that they can't see, but that impact them greatly. Emotional intelligence is a skill that everyone can learn, we just need a place to start. The important things to learn at this level are:

1. What are the six families of emotions.

2. Of the two fear buckets, scared is fear of the present, and anxiety is fear of the future.

3. Emotions are not good or bad, they just are, and if we learn to control them they can eventually be our superpower.

# Level Three (proficient)

This is where we start to learn about the importance of controlling the intensity of emotion. Many adults never get beyond level one, so anyone trying to apply this for the first time should start at level three. The older people are, the quicker they tend to move to level five and seven. The three most important things to note at level three are:

1.  We have words to help explain different levels of intensity of each emotion.

2.  Words in the centre of the circle are when we are out of control, and we need to know how to dial it back to the outer rim if we want to stay in control of our actions.

3.  You can match appropriate intensity to different situations. For example, It's okay to be disappointed you missed out on the food you wanted, but it's not okay to be in despair. It's okay to be worried about an exam coming up if it motivates you to study, which is more appropriate than being overwhelmed about it (which is de-motivating).

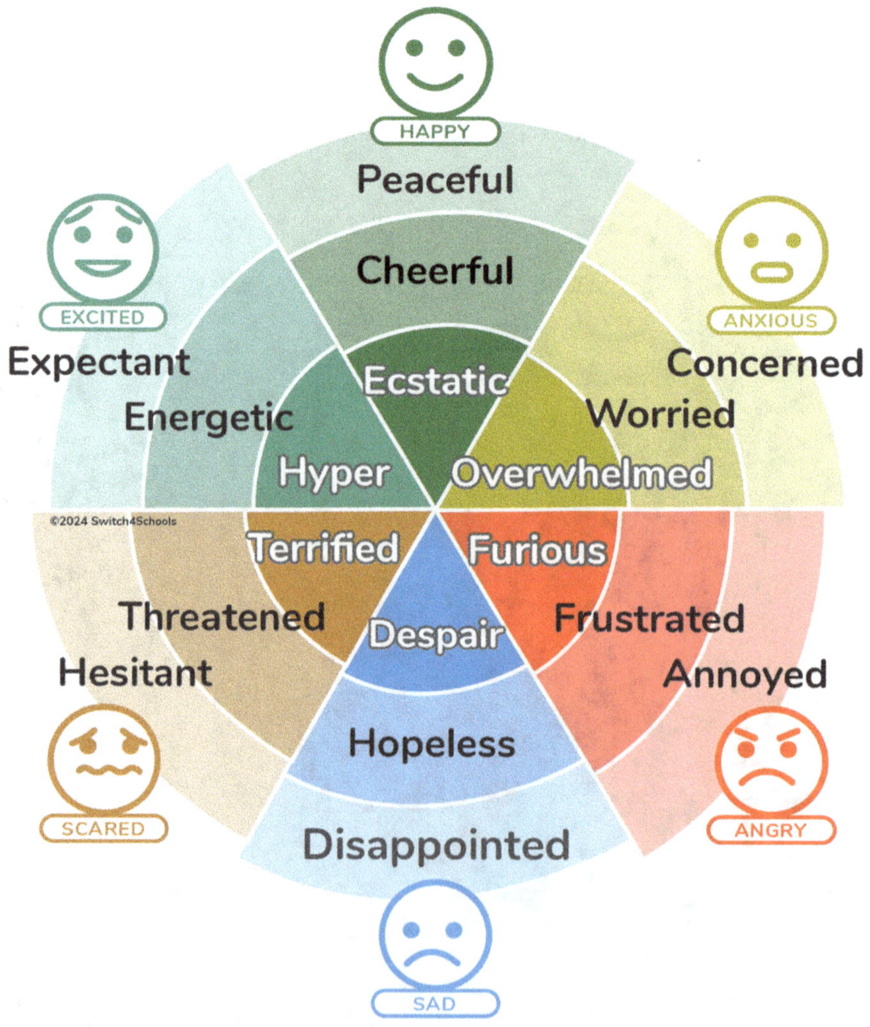

# Level Five (advanced)

Level five is where it really starts to get interesting. Here there are enough words to start to have enough levels to 'dial it up' when you need to, and can start to notice the nuances in the escalation of other people's behaviour. It is also complex enough for you to start to experiment with more advanced applications of emotions, such as empathy and motivation. The three most important things to note at level five are:

1. There are subtle ways we can dial up the intensity of emotion without losing control.

2. We can feel different emotions at once, and can jump between emotional states quite quickly at times (i.e. energetic can quickly turn into frustration, worry into eagerness).

3. You don't need to be happy all the time, but simply being peaceful is a version of happiness. The pursuit of happiness is actually the pursuit of peace.

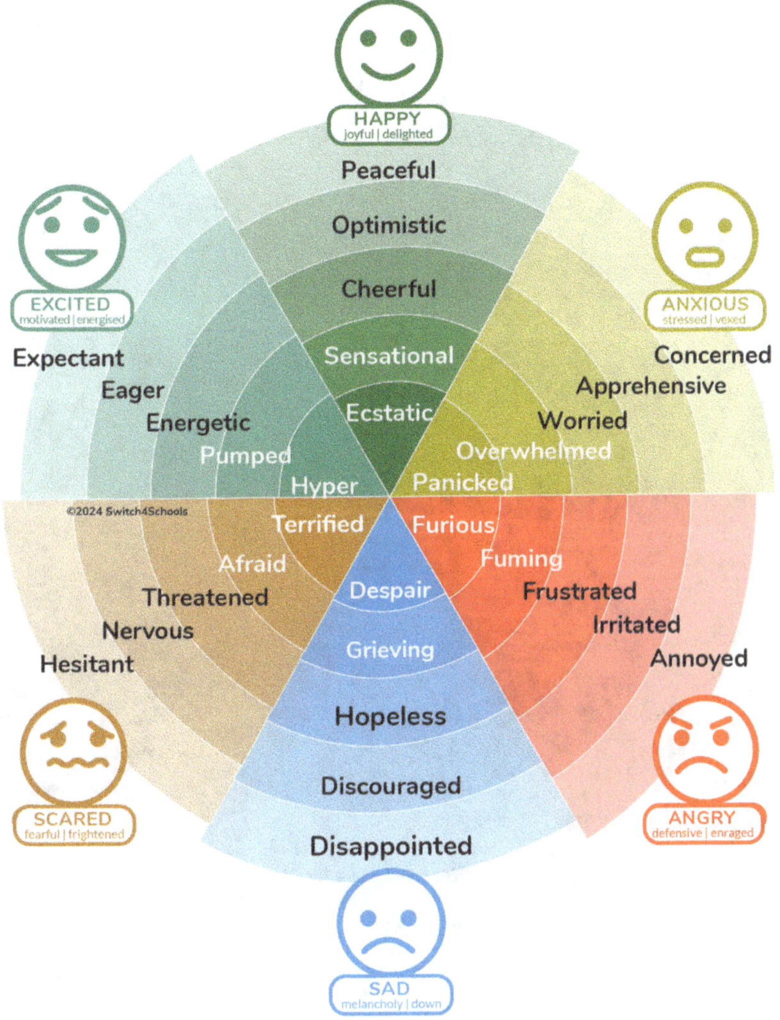

# Level Seven (mastery)

Now we are using and managing emotion in ourselves and others. You can spend a lifetime mastering emotion at this level. Here you learn the emotions are critical in making decisions, motivating action and building a successful life. The three most important things to note at level seven are:

1.  You can feel multiple emotions at once. Happiness and sadness are not opposites. It is possible to be grieving and at peace at the same time.

2.  There are times (like preparing for a big event) where you can harness high intensity emotion to move yourself and others toward action. Knowing when and how to dial it back so you don't stay there for too long is critical.

3.  Trying to be rational with others when they are highly aroused will not work. Learning to identify when people have 'lost their mind', and knowing how to help them dial it up and down is a master skill.

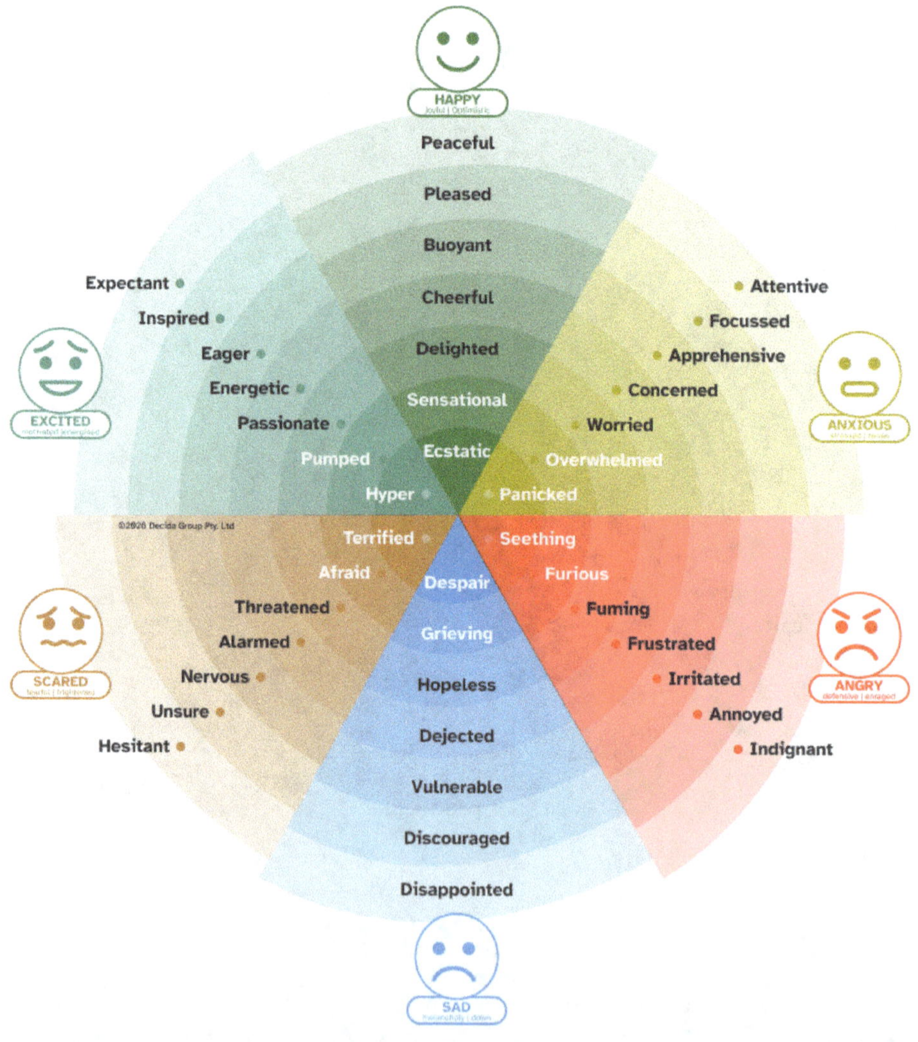

For the rest of these pages, the rest of this book,

we will talk through emotion, lift the lid,
have a look.

When you find something little that resonates
with you,

take a note, make a mark, take some time to think it
through.

For only when we take time to follow
our curiosity,

do we give ourselves the space to learn, to live,
to see.

## ANGRY

defensive | enraged

## EXCITED

motivated | energised

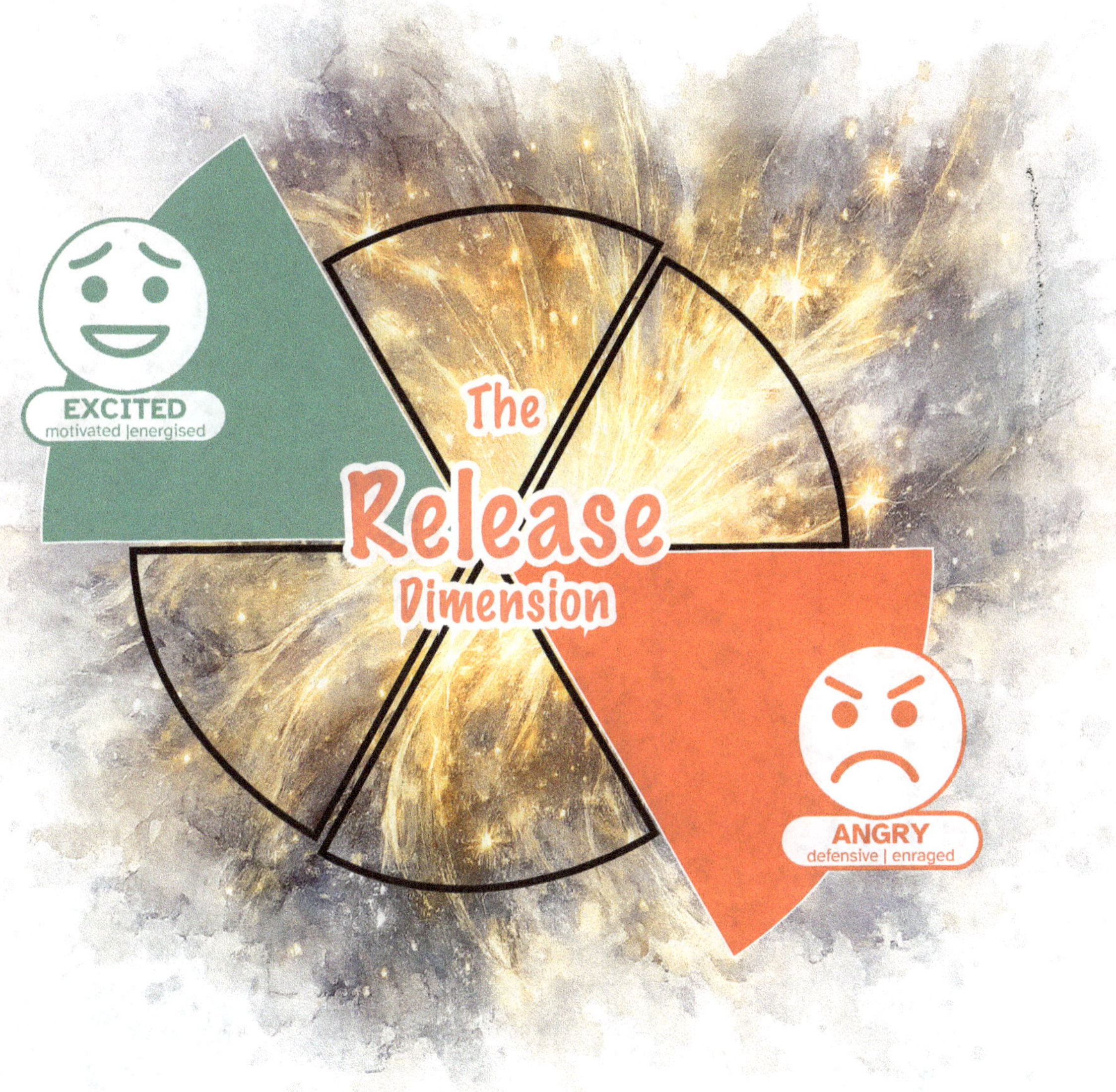


On the Switch Emotion Wheel™, anger and excitement sit side by side because they are both ways we release built-up emotional energy. When pressure from fear, sadness, or anxiety builds, it has to come out somewhere. For some people, it comes out as anger. For others, it shows up as excitement. The energy is the same, the outlet is different.

The skill is learning to direct that energy. Excitement can also be used to reframe high levels of anxiety or scared, a trick commonly used in high performance sports. Instead of being nervous or overwhelmed by an upcoming race, they are eager to get out there, full of anticipation, pumped for the challenge ahead. This redirects the energy toward a more productive mindset, increasing performance and interrupting unhelpful rumination.

The goal isn't to eliminate anger or excitement, but to use it well. Direct it appropriately. Emotional energy will be released either way. Emotional agency lets you choose how.

# ANGRY
defensive | enraged

# Summary

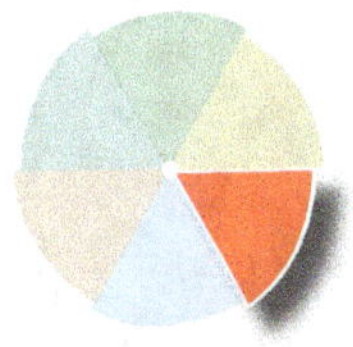

Anger is a very strong, action-oriented emotion that can lead you to doing things that you may later regret.

Physically lashing out at someone in anger can mean that you hurt someone, or say some pretty horrible and hurtful things. You mostly feel anger when someone has hurt you, treated you unfairly, or gets in the way of completing a task.

## When does it help?

Anger can help us stand up for ourselves, protect ourselves and those we love, and help get us out of a dangerous situation. Learning how to be angry without flipping into fury, controlling and releasing the energy in a way that keeps your rational brain in control, is so important.

## What happens inside my body?

### hands

grab a weapon or strike enemy

### adrenaline

pulsing energy strong enough for vigorous action

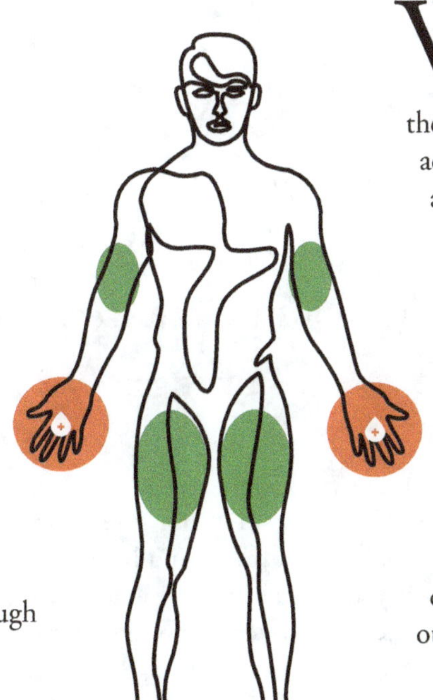

When we start to feel angry, our body directs blood to the hands and the chemical adrenalin is pumped to our arms and legs. This is our body readying ourselves to fend off an attack from an unfriendly, or remove something (or someone) that might be in the way of us getting to safety.

Often when angry, we will clench fists or fold arms in response to the blood and chemicals pulsing through our body.

**ANGRY**
defensive | enraged

# Indignant

*In control, but injustice noted.*

> *"There is a power that can be created out of pent-up indignation, courage, and the inspiration of a common cause... It is a phenomenon recorded again and again in the history of popular movements against injustice all over the world."*
>
> - Howard Zinn

**Indignant** · Annoyed · Irritated · Frustrated · Fuming · Furious · Seething

A little bit ——————→ Extreme

Indignant describes the lowest arousal of anger below annoyed.

It is a light anger usually felt when you lose your dignity, or observe someone else unfairly losing theirs. This unfair treatment is first met with indignance, and if the issue isn't addresses the perceived injustice can escalate quickly to higher levels of anger.

Being indignant results in someone saying, "I'm not sure that's right" or, "that's a bit unfair isn't it?" It is usually shown in the face as a frown and looking directly at the thing or person who is judged to be acting unfairly. Importantly there is always a level of curiosity at this level, wanting to confirm if the unfairness is justified or if there may be a misinterpretation. This is a learning mindset. If one is convinced of a miscarriage of justice, anger will usually escalate to higher arousal levels.

# Annoyed

*Still in control, but distracted by something.*

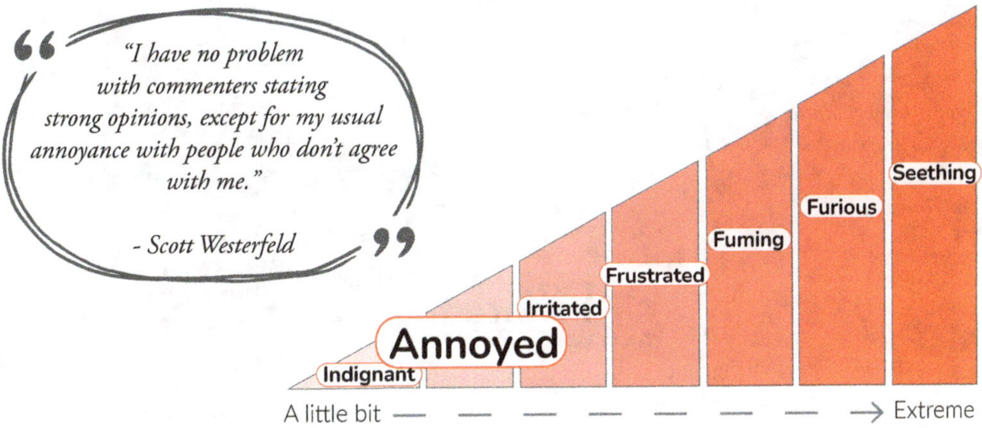


A mild and somewhat tempered version of anger.

"I am annoyed at myself / someone else / something for interfering with my expectations". Being annoyed can quickly turn into irritation or frustration if the thing (or person) you are annoyed at continues. If you are unable to confront or deal with the annoyance, over time it can lead to feelings of resentment.

Annoyance is a fleeting emotion that shouldn't hang around for too long. Often it doesn't register on your face or have a huge impact on your daily life. It tends to be an 'eye rolling' moment that goes as quickly as it comes. Learning to deal with things that you find annoying in people you love can require developing good negotiation skills.

# Irritated

*In control, but focus is on the irritant.*

> *"... nothing winds me up more than people saying, 'Chill out' to me when I'm irritated!"*
>
> - Martin Freeman

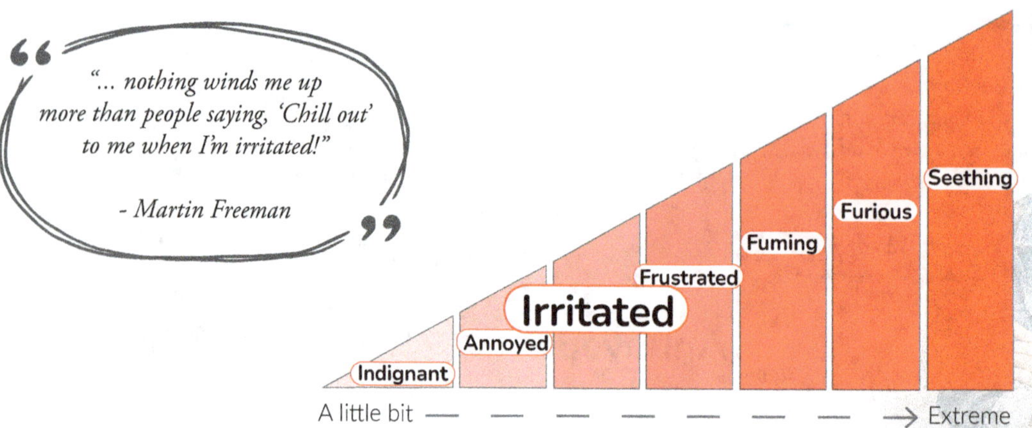



Irritated is a step up from being annoyed, but is still a relatively mild form of anger.

When you are irritated you have a strong desire to remove the irritation—it is not something easily ignored. Irritations are a little painful, and the brain interprets pain as a warning signal for something needing to be fixed. If the irritation isn't dealt with, people often get forthright or aggressive in an attempt to resolve the pain.

Constant irritation can make you impatient, and will turn into frustration if it distracts or is a barrier to you achieving something important. Often irritations are met with a stern frown. They are things that are small enough not to lose control over, but are too big to ignore.

# Frustrated

*On the edge of losing control.*

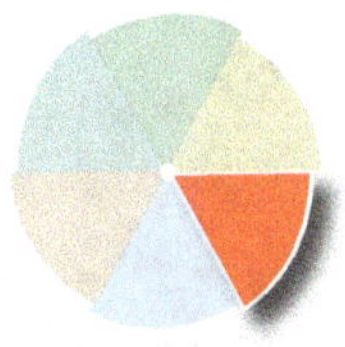

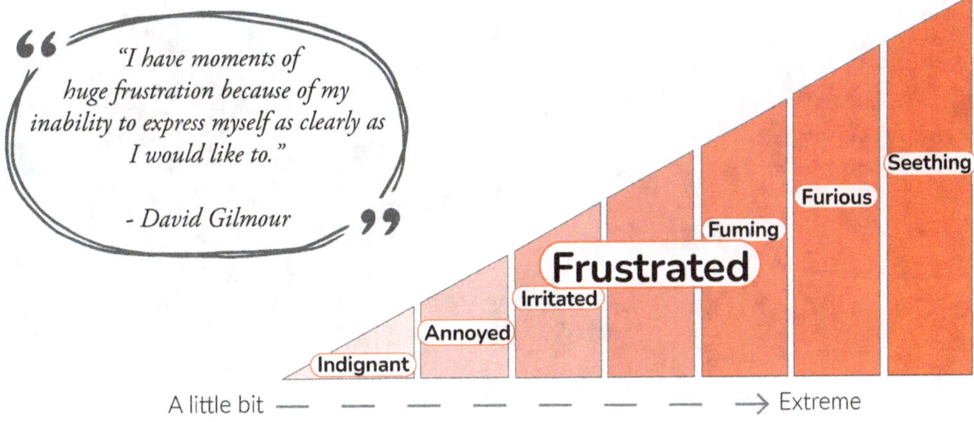


Frustration is where anger can start to boil over into something harder to control.

Usually it is triggered when something gets in the way of achieving a specific goal or completing a task. "They couldn't understand what I was saying, it was getting frustrating". Frustration is an emotion that is very hard to suppress, and rarely considers future negative impacts of outbursts.

Frustration is a strong emotion that can often lead to lashing out physically or verbally. It can be more explosive if the frustrating 'thing' happens close to you achieving your goal, or when you're desperate to get something (e.g. waiting in line for an hour to get some food, only to have someone push in front of you as you finally get to the counter).

# Fuming

*Losing control, high energy used to keep in check.*

> "I was fuming with anger, quietly spending all my energy suppressing the rage that was building inside. I tried to give a reassuring smile, but it was clear I was fuming inside."
>
> - Tim Edals

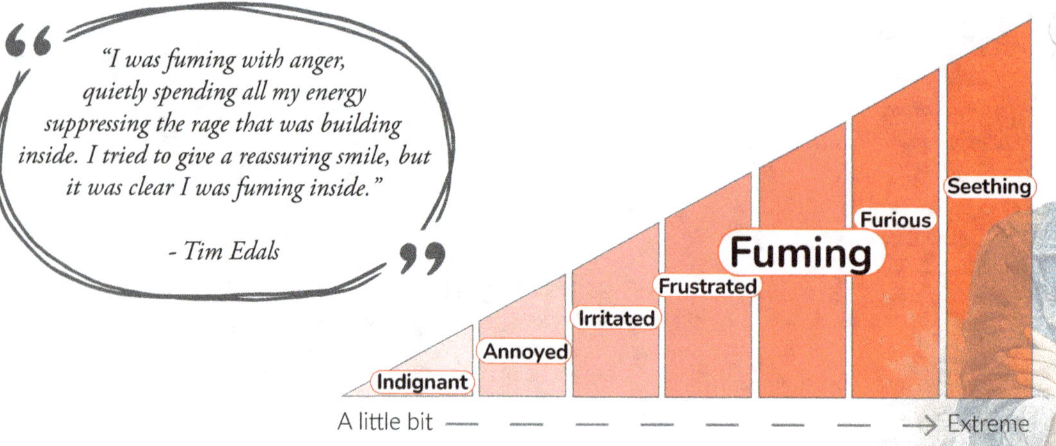


Fuming is a very strong emotion.

It is often triggered by perceived social injustice, people ignoring you, people not keeping their word, forced change, or general disrespect. It is also strongly related to unforgiveness and revenge. When you are fuming you stop listening to anyone, get caught in long rants, and hold aggressive postures (like pointing, clenching fists, or shaking your head).

While it can still feel like you are in control when you are fuming, you are not. Your rational brain may be conscious of what you are doing (unlike furious), but awareness will have little to no control over your behaviour. Learning and practicing grace, humility, compassion and forgiveness is critical to controlling this emotion.

# Furious

*No control, prone to irrational outbursts.*

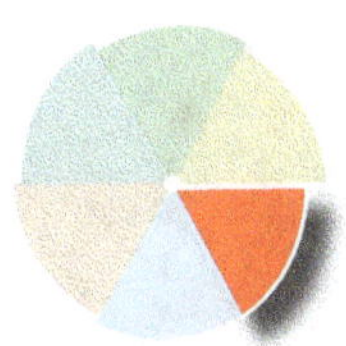

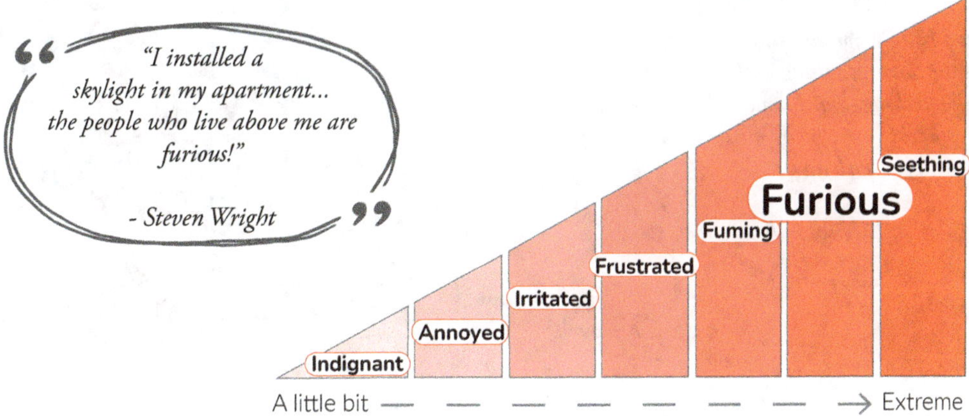


Fury is an extremely strong expression of anger.

People often lose control of their thoughts, actions or words when they are consumed with fury. People become furious when something about their core identity feels threatened. People who commit violent crimes often report 'losing their mind' in fits of rage, unable to even remember what they did or why they did it.

Your rational brain slips into a semi-conscious state as your entire body becomes engulfed in fury, with the impact of your uncontrolled behaviour often leading to deep remorse after you've calmed down. Work on dialling back your anger to annoyed when you feel yourself creep toward fury.

# Seething

*Completely out of control, prone to psychological harm.*

> *"In the cases I study, you sometimes have someone who is seething with anger... I want something, and I am entitled to get what I want, and if you thwart me it really makes me seeth with anger."*
>
> *- Psychologist, David Lisak*

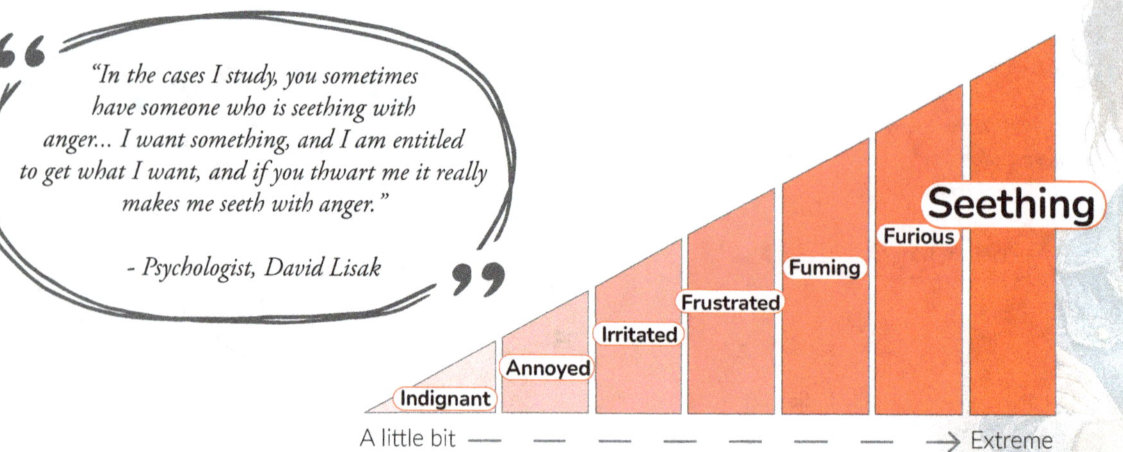


This is 'white hot' anger.

Often people 'spit' words through clenched teeth, giving rise to the seething sound of hissing. However, most times people hide this anger away, cutting others off, disregarding them, or acting in passive aggressive ways.

Seething is an extreme expression of anger and one should refrain from speaking or acting out in this state. However, you also need to make sure you deal with the anger, and find ways to expel it so that it doesn't percolate. Holding on to seething anger will lead to psychological pain, and will hurt you much more than the person you're are seething over. While you may be able to put the seething anger out of you mind to focus on a specific task or goal, it will be in the background draining energy as you try to keep it suppressed. Being gracious, quick to forgive, and holding things lightly is a much better way to manage this level of anger.

# EXCITED
motivated | energised

# Summary

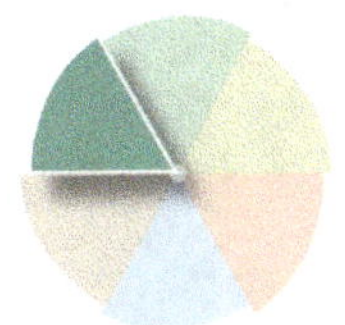

Excitement, like anger, is how we often release energy. It's a series of emotions that usually result from something in the future that amuses or interests you. You can feel excited about going on a holiday, falling in love, or seeing the sequel to a great movie. Excitement is related to happiness, but happiness is directed toward something happening in the present, whereas excitement is all about the anticipation of a future event.

## When does it help?

Excitement boosts motivation levels so we can be prepared. It also can be a helpful way to reframe anxiety — instead of being stressed about your upcoming event, you can think about being full of anticipation and excitement. This subtle mindset change can refocus your energy and increase performance (rather than the decrease we see with high anxiety).

## What happens inside my body?

### large skeletal muscles

easier for prolonged activity

### adrenaline

'energy' that often needs to be burnt off by jumping, shaking or thrill seeking (achievement satisfaction)

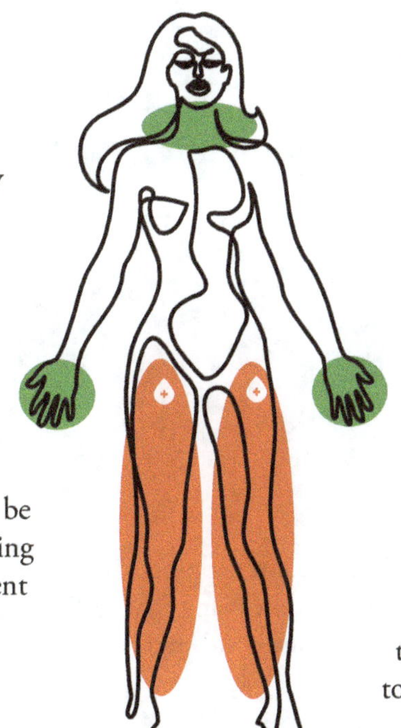

The heart will be racing and you may find yourself naturally jumping up and down, clapping vigorously, or even screaming in delight in an attempt to release the energy excitement brings.

Blood pumps to all your 'action' muscles, allowing you to do activities (like dancing) for a long time. It can also stimulate creative and pleasurable thoughts about the future. Too much excitement can interrupt your sleep in similar ways to anxiety, so learning some ways to calm your mind before going to sleep can be good.

# Expectant

*In control, feeling good about the something immediately about to happen.*

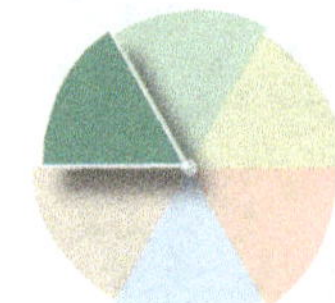

> "*Each day is a blessing. Be expectant and have faith that one day, your miracles will manifest.*"
>
> *- Gift Gugu Mona*

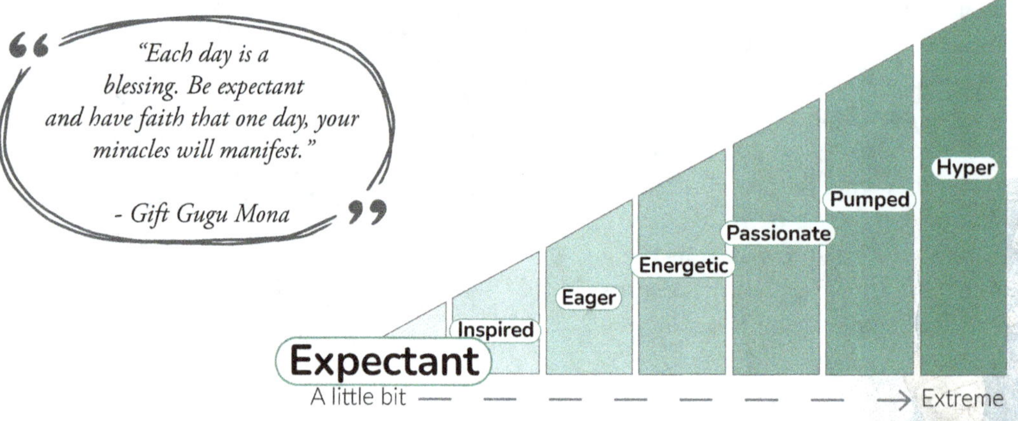


Being expectant is one of the most enjoyable emotions as it creates energy and joy through low levels of excitement.

It is often articulated as "looking forward to" something - like a holiday, a party, or a new year. People who are expressing excitement via expectant feelings tend to be active and feel 'lighter', which is expressed through raised eyebrows and a slight smile.

Joy is often articulated as a mix of low levels of happiness and low levels of excitement. Learning what being expectant feels like, and then accessing that feeling whenever you need it, can be useful if needing to shift out of an anxious or sad state.

# Inspired

*Starting to move toward desired goal.*

*"Concern yourself more with accepting responsibility than with assigning blame. Let the possibilities inspire you more than the obstacles discourage you."*

*- Ralph Marston*

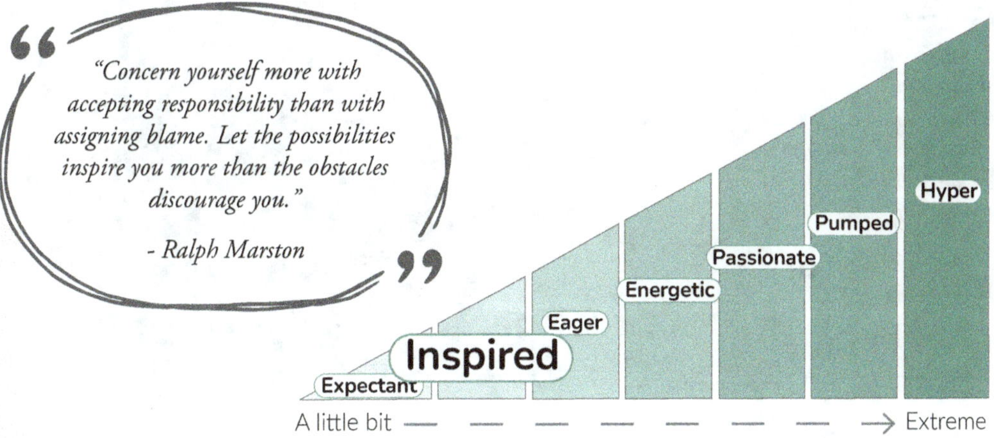


Inspired is greater than expectant, and it is often mixed with a sense of wonder and enhanced possibility.

Inspiration can come through beauty, symmetry, another person's words or actions, or even the realisation that you can solve a problem. Feeling inspired is mostly associated with creating a better future.

Inspiration has long been used as a tool for motivation, partly because it is a strong enough emotion to nudge action, without draining too much energy. This means that someone who is inspired by something can remain on task for an extended period of time without getting mentally exhausted. This can become extremely powerful when mixed with other low arousal emotions such as focused (anxiety).

# Eager

*Still in control, keen to experience a good outcome.*

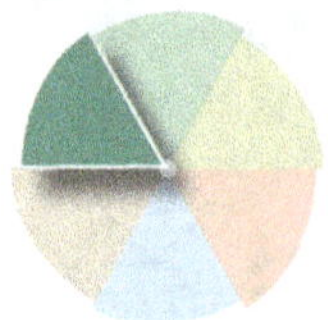

> *"As kids we didn't complain about being poor; we talked about how rich we were going to be... And as soon as we had a little money, we were eager to show it."*
>
> *- Jay Z*

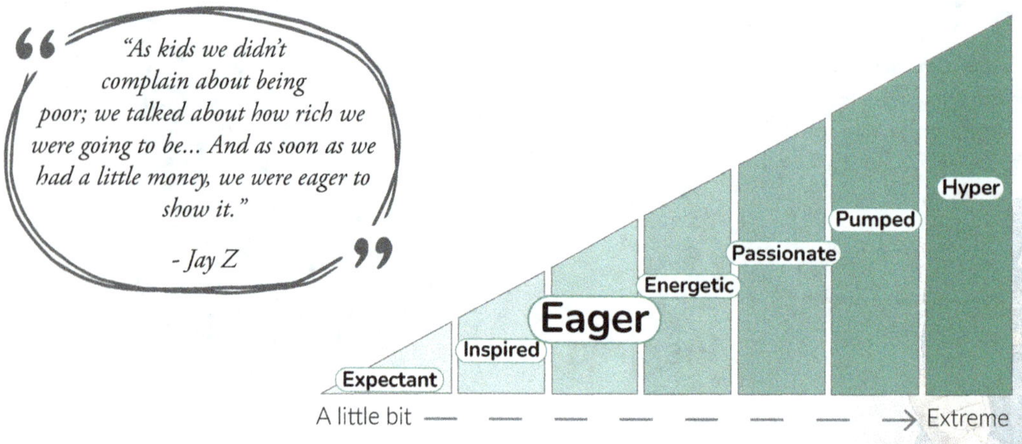


Eager is more intense than expectant, but falls a little short of the higher arousal state of energetic.

People who are eager will often clap or rub their hands to release energy, or 'bob' up and down on their toes. Eagerness is often experienced when an event that you've been looking forward to is about to happen, or you are impatient and desire to get to a destination or complete a task sooner than later. It is a great way to focus energy toward an action.

Saying you're 'eager' (which leads to action and enthusiasm) can be an easy way of reframing worry or panic (which can undermine performance and sleep) or impatience (which can lead to frustration and anger). Learning how to feel and trigger eagerness is one of the superpowers of high performers.

# Energetic

*The tipping point of ceding control.*

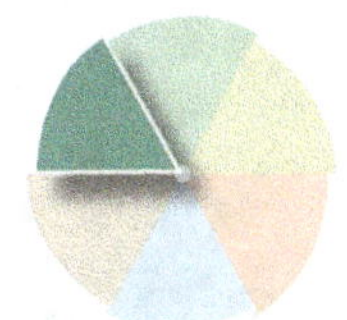

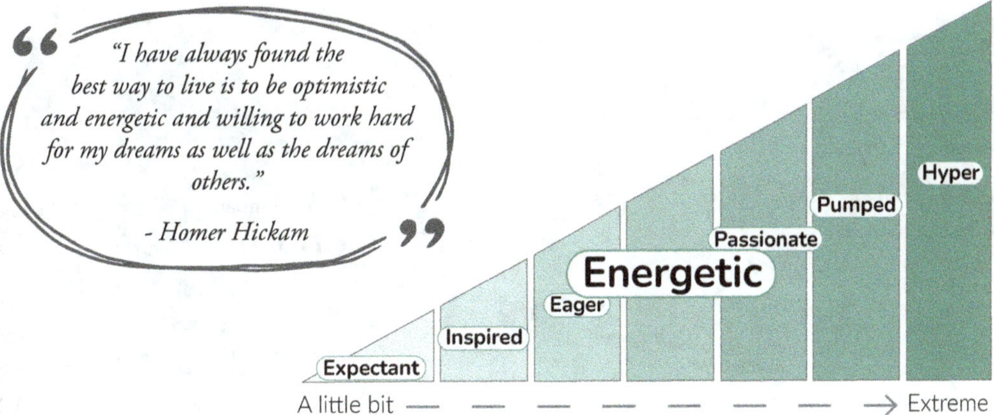


Feeling energetic is more than simply being eager to do something—it is a high energy state that readies the body for imminent action.

Being energetic causes people to move quicker, or focus intently on what they are energetic about (often ignoring other inconsequential things). An energetic person has a happy but intense look, and speech patterns tend to be faster, louder, and more expressive.

Energetic is a highly contagious emotion as long as others are also energised by the same activity. If not, then people seeing your energetic state can view you as disturbing the peace or creating extra work. This is no reason not to be energetic, but be mindful of the impact on others and general politics of social environments where possible.

# Passionate

*In flow, unaware of all of your surroundings.*

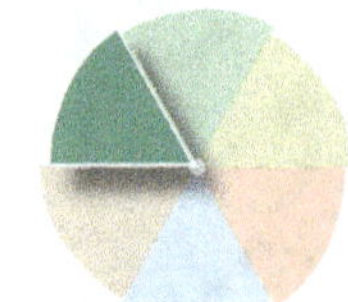

> "I have no special talent. I am only passionately curious."
>
> - Albert Einstein

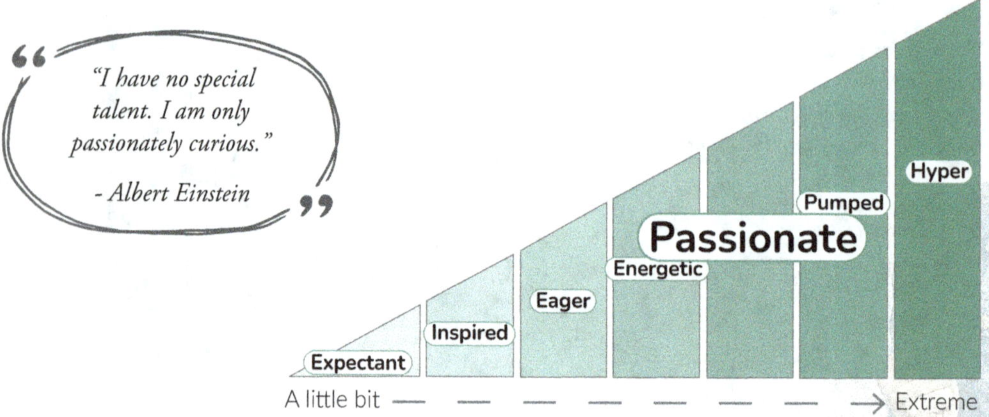


When you are passionate, you are excited almost to the point of being out of control.

Passionate can sometimes look like fury (anger) due to its high intensity, passionate people can easily slip into frustration if someone, or something, is a blocker to achieving their passion. Other people are often attracted to passionate people because this level of energy can be contagious, temporarily lifting mood.

There is an element of passion that is not welcomed by others. As the arousal level suggests, people full of passion are not always in control of their actions, and can be blind to things that may hamper their future success. Others can see passion as simply over-opinionated or pushy. It is important to feel passionate about things (like if you are on stage performing, competing in sport, or arguing a political point), but knowing how to quickly dial it down and increase awareness is important so you don't exhaust yourself or the people around you.

# Pumped

*Highly reactive and energetic, relying on automatic behaviours and thinking.*

> *"Sometimes I get so pumped up, I get a headache. I get woozy. I get dizzy. I like that feeling, I don't know why."*
>
> *- Torii Hunter*

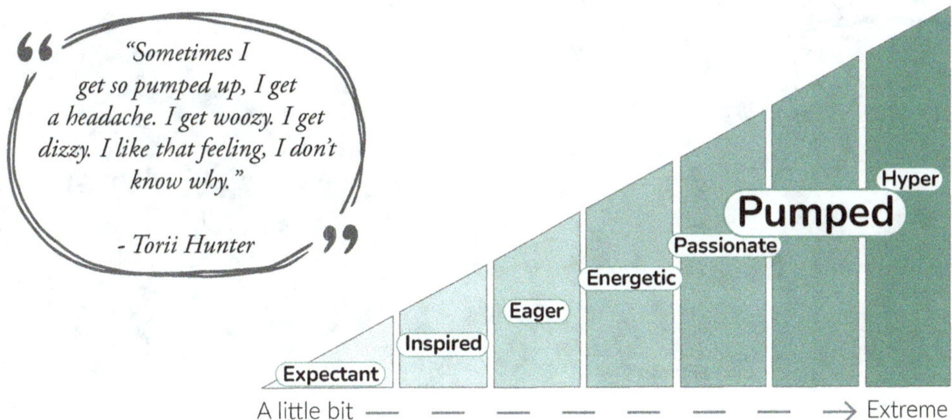


Pumped is a colloquial expression used to articulate high energy and excitement toward an imminent event or action.

Unsustainable as a long-term emotion, it can be useful to rally behind a cause or put in extra effort where needed to win. The intense look of someone feeling pumped is reflected in furrowed brows, and often loud clapping or vocalisations (e.g. "Woohoo!" "Yeah!" "C'mon!").

Music or motivational speeches before undertaking a daunting task can help get people 'pumped up' and override fear and anxiety. Learning how to feel pumped can help overcome procrastination, particularly for a task that is boring or requires a lot of effort. Just be aware that trying to stay in this state for too long will be exhausting.

# Hyper

*Out of control, no ability to keep enthusiasm.*

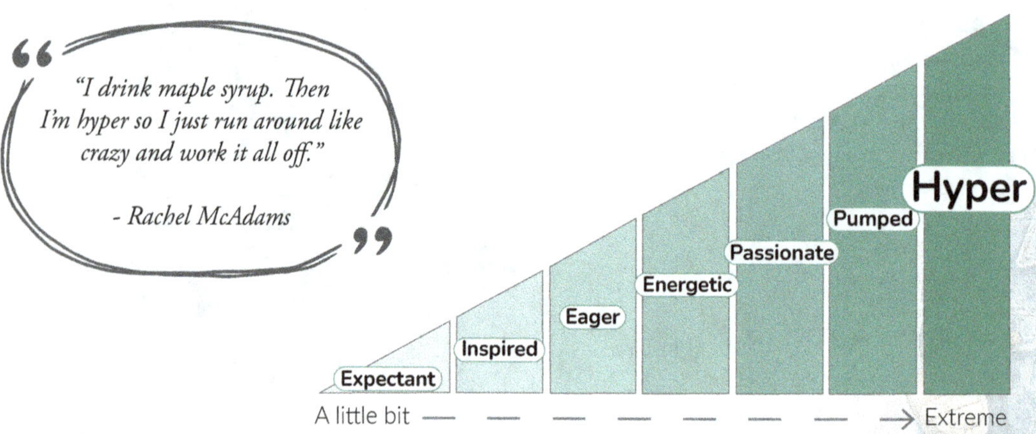


Hyper (also called hyperactivity) is the most energetic and extreme expression of excitement.

Hyper tends to be a result of an overabundance of internal energy that needs to be released. In a hyper state, people are loud, distractable and highly active. They can be socially disruptive and chaotic, and rarely focus on a particular outcome. Hyper can easily turn to anger if others try to mute or suppress the disruptive behaviour.

Being hyped for long periods of time is unlikely to result in good outcomes. When in a hyper state you lose rational control and you can have a significant negative impact on those around you without realising it. Learning to breathe, focus, and redirect energy toward more controlled expressions (like playing sport) can be a good way to keep energy high, without going over the top.

# ANXIOUS
stressed | vexed

# SCARED
fearful | frightened

Feeling anxious and feeling scared are both forms of fear, but they point to different things. Scared is about a threat right now. Anxious is about a threat that might happen later. That difference matters, because it changes how your body reacts and how you manage it.

Both are tied to our built-in survival system, often called the five F's: freeze, flop, fawn, fight, or flight. These are fast, automatic responses to perceived danger, even when the threat only exists in our thoughts.

The key skill is not just calming these reactions down, but knowing when to use them. A bit of anxiety can help you prepare, focus, and perform. Feeling scared can sharpen your response when something genuinely needs your attention. Emotional agency is about being able to dial that intensity up when it's useful, and back down when it's not.

When you can do that, you're no longer just reacting to fear. You're using it.

# ANXIOUS

stressed | vexed

# Summary

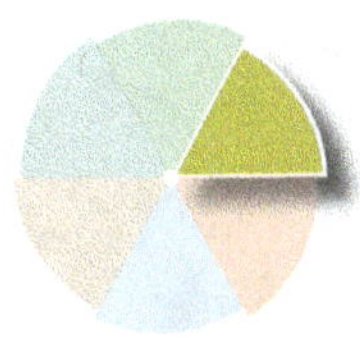

Anxiety is a stress response to something negative or dangerous that we think might happen in the future. It differs from scared which tends to be felt in response to something dangerous in the present. Anxiety can impact our breathing and our ability to sleep. Ruminating and constantly visualising potential future negative events can actually help make them happen, further fueling anxiety.

## When does it help?

Anxiety can help us remain vigilant to potential threats and help direct attention to important things. Being anxious about school grades can help us focus on studying. Being anxious about health can help us exercise or eat a better diet. Only be anxious about the things you can control, and don't fall into the trap of over-vigilance.

***The Switch4Schools app has some handy hints for sleeping and calming the mind.***

## What happens inside my body?

### heart, large muscles

large muscles and heart dilate, increasing blood pressure - 'overcooked' organs reduce performance

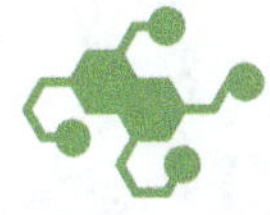

### adrenaline, noradrenaline, cortisol

(stress hormones) increasing vigilance and sensitivity to environmental changes

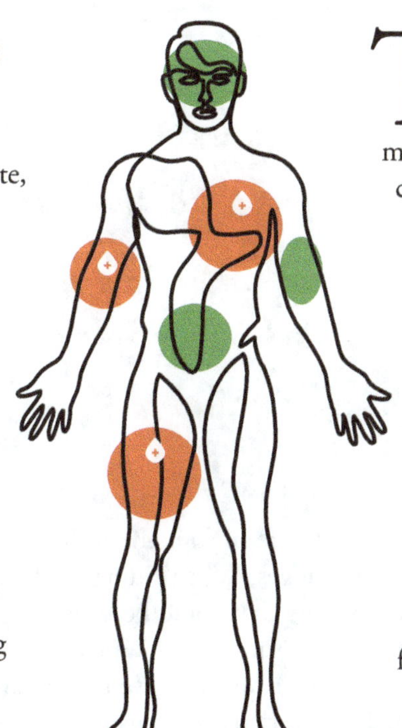

The stress hormones in your stomach can feel like 'butterflies', or even make you start to feel sick. This can be why anxious people eat comfort food or start to eat less, because they are trying to make their stomach feel good. As blood is directed away from your hands and feet, they can become clammy and sweaty. Your heart starts racing as it pumps blood to arms and leg muscles, often tiring them out due to over-stimulation and making you feel like you have no energy.

# Attentive

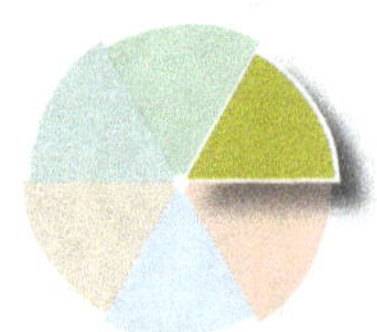

*In control, potential threat noted.*



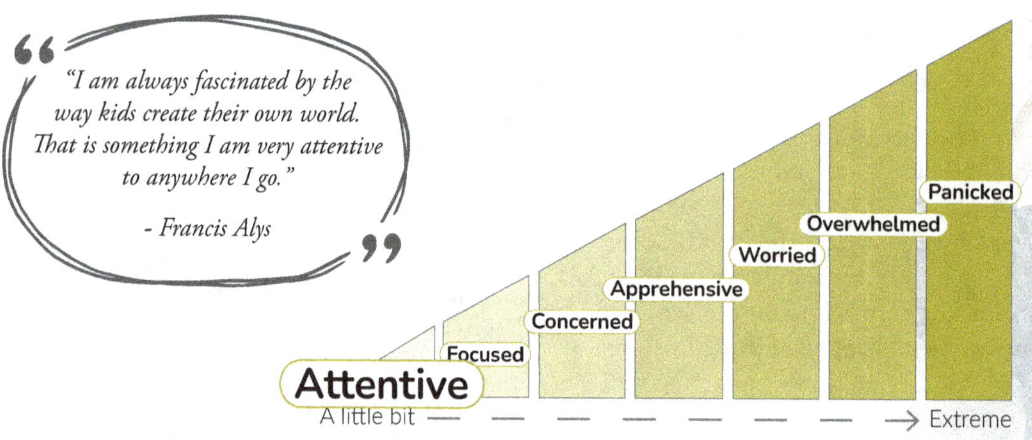


The lower arousal end of anxiety is most useful.

It motivates us to focus on things that are important and solve problems that need solving. Attentiveness is when our brain identifies something that might be problematic in the future, but it's not confirmed as a definite future problem - so we just monitor it.

Think of this like simply taking mental note of something that could become a future problem, and keeping an eye on it to see if it changes. When riding a bike it is important to be attentive to your surroundings to identify anything that could become dangerous, but rarely does it need anything more than this if you are on a leisurely ride. When cooking you are attentive to sounds and smells that could indicate something is burning, even if you are not visually focused on it at the time. This very low level of anxiety is very useful to navigating the world safely, when speaking in front of a group of people, monitoring your health, or to avoid procrastination.

# Focused

*Working on avoiding negative future outcomes.*

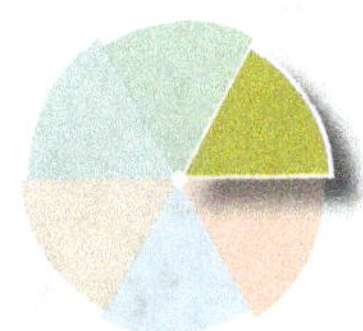

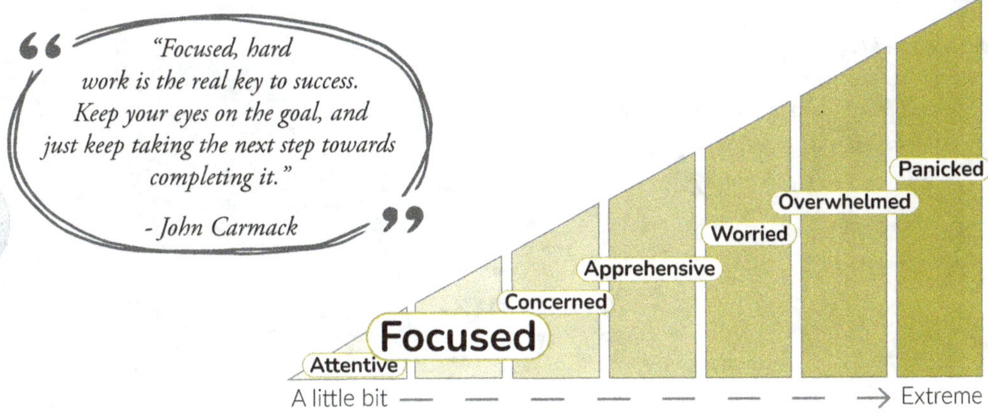


Once something changes from being a possible problem, to a probable problem, we move from attentive to focused.

Here is when we direct our attention to fix something in order to avoid future problems. Something deserves your focused attention and if you start to lose control of the situation you start to feel concerned.

Being in this state of focus can sometimes be referred to as being 'in flow'. There is enough stress to motivate you to lose yourself in what you are doing, without the task draining too much of your energy. When 'in flow', people often report losing track of time, and being able to work non-stop for very long periods of time. In the workplace, keeping people in this light state of anxiety can dramatically improve productivity and even morale. People in this state often feel like their work is meaningful, and report high levels of satisfaction when a job is complete.

# Concerned

*Questioning actions and thoughts, attention is directed toward potential danger.*

*"I am concerned for the security of our great nation; not so much because of any threat from without, but because of the insidious forces working from within."*

*- Douglas MacArthur*

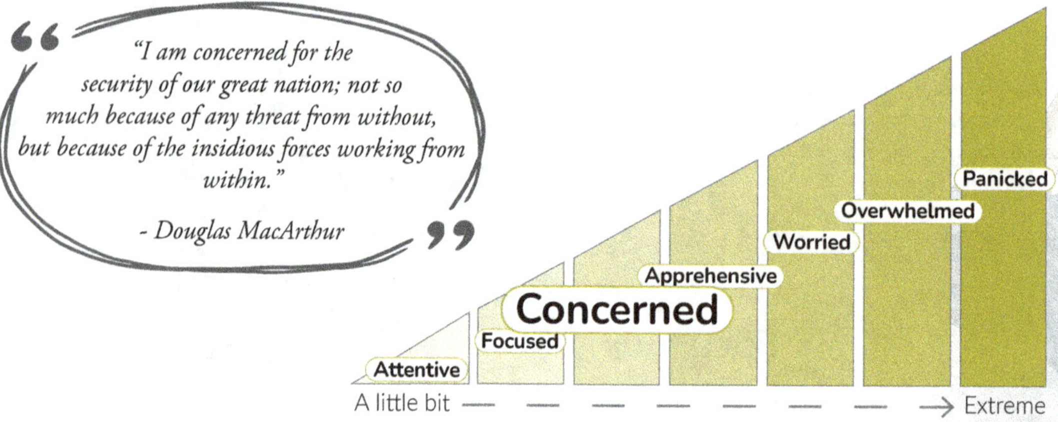


When things or issues start to feel out of control or uncertain, you can feel concerned.

Being concerned helps focus your unconscious mind to either monitor or solve problems while you are doing other things. A lot of concern tends to revolve around health, money, success, or relationships.

The act of being concerned means examining something in the present that could have a negative outcome in the future. You are concerned with things in your immediate control. If you are focusing on something that may only happen in the future you are more likely to be worried rather than simply concerned.

# Apprehensive

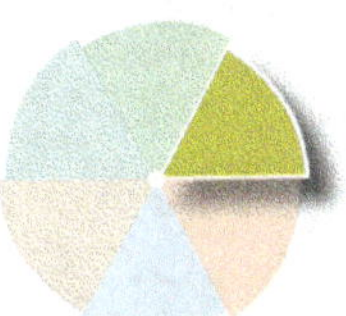

*On the cusp of losing control, need to address an issue.*

> *"I had become shy of life's bustle in my solitary retreat and was apprehensive at the thought of facing the world."*
>
> *- Selma Lagerlof*

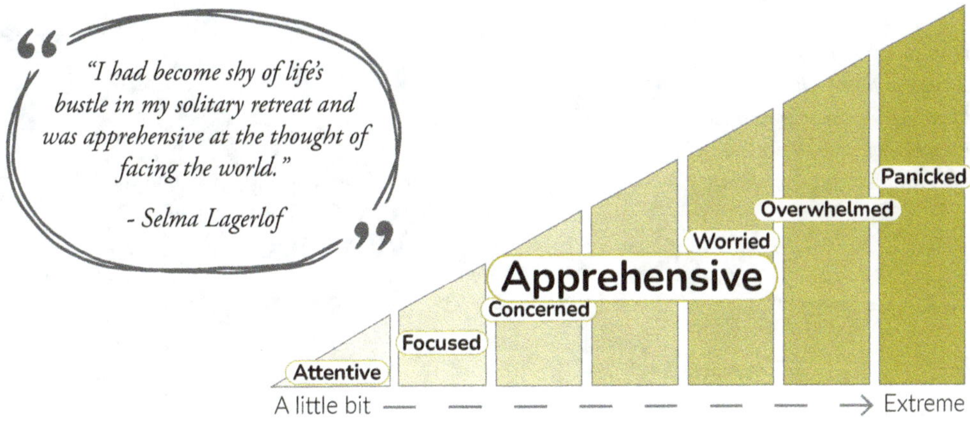


Apprehension is a mid-level arousal emotional state that focuses your attention toward something in the present that you think is likely to become problematic in the future.

Being apprehensive causes your brow to furrow and your attention to dart around a little to maintain alertness and avoid danger.  Apprehension stems from being uncertain about consequences of actions.

Concerned and apprehensive can be useful emotional expressions of anxiety, which help you plan for unexpected events and deal with issues before they become major problems. Be careful not to fall into the trap that you can only be safe if constantly vigilant, which keeps us in higher expressions of anxiety, robs us of feeling good about being peaceful, and blinds us to good things in the present.

# Worried

*A future problem must be resolved, capturing the mind.*

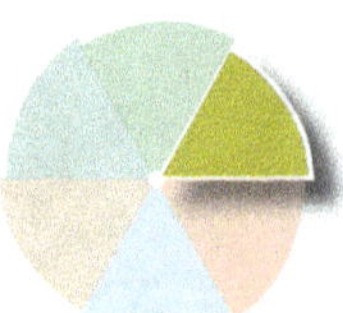

> "Fear keeps us focused on the past or worried about the future. If we can acknowledge our fear, we can realise that right now we are okay. Right now, today, we are still alive, and our bodies are working marvelously."
>
> - Thich Nhat Hanh

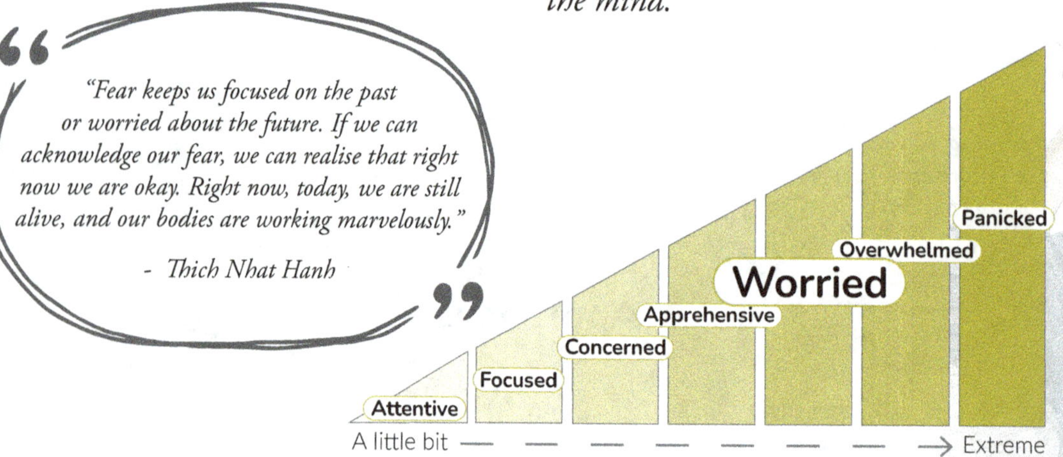


Worry is what you feel about a future event that you feel you have little or no control over.

It has a relatively high energy state so the body will often move around (like pacing up and down) in order to release energy and stimulate thought. It is not healthy to remain worried, as it tends to concern things out of our control or imaginary future states.

Don't worry, be happy. The popular song written by Bobby McFerrin holds a lot of truth. Even 2000 years ago it was written in the Bible, "Do not worry about tomorrow, for tomorrow will worry about itself. Each day has enough trouble of its own". Most of the time and energy spent worrying is simply wasted energy. It's good to have a plan and make yourself more resilient to future issues, but don't let worry run the show. Direct your energy into things that will positively impact today.

# Overwhelmed

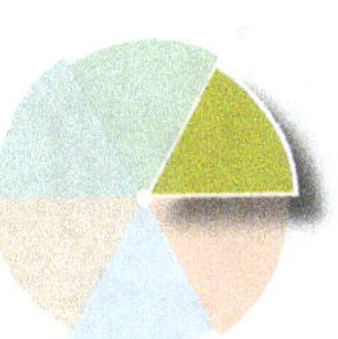

*Lost control of all rational thought, desperately seeking exit.*

*"Pray when you feel overwhelmed and anxious. Do not be anxious about anything, but in every situation, by prayer and petition, with thanksgiving, present your requests to God."*

*- Philippians 4:6-7*

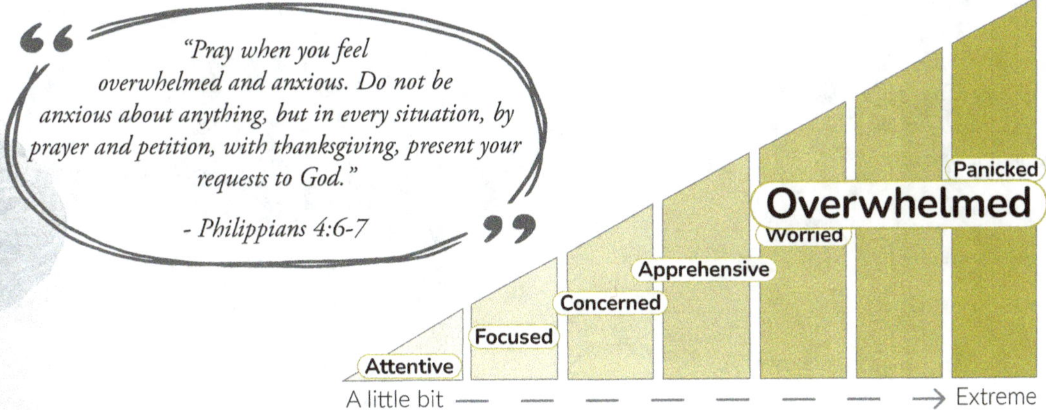


When anxiety gets out of control we become confused and overwhelmed.

People in this expression of anxiety often need to seek external help to manage their anxiety and get back in control of their thoughts and actions. Overwhelmed is charaterised by deep frowning, scattered and irrational speech, an inability to engage in certain social situations, insomnia and an inability to quieten the mind.

People can be triggered into overwhelm and panic by projecting negative memories onto future scenarios, or even fear of being judged, failing, or looking unintelligent. Overwhelm and panic reduces performance and makes difficult situations worse. Learning to dial it back to concern is critical in it's management.

# Panicked

*Completely out of control, actions and thoughts erratic and irrational.*

> *"Panic causes tunnel vision. Calm acceptance of danger allows us to more easily assess the situation and see the options."*
>
> *- Simon Sinek*

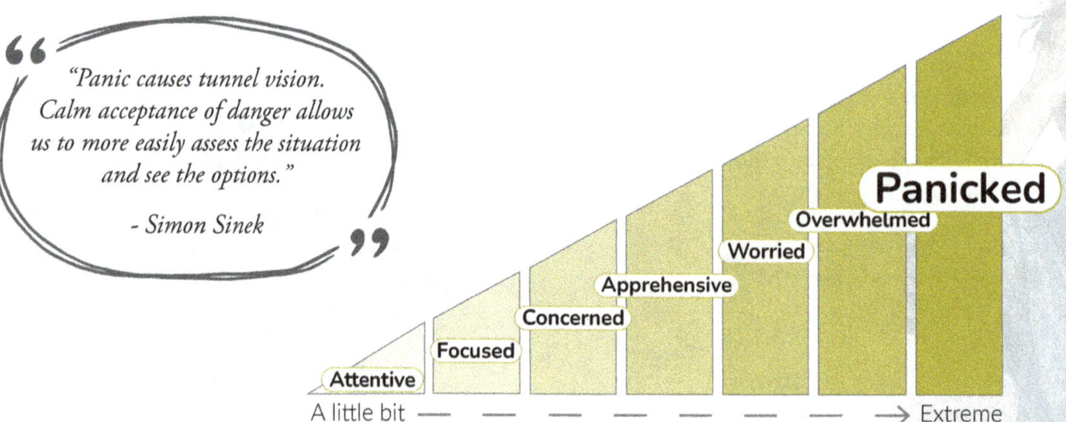


When anxiety reaches it's highest level, we panic.

Panic is a high energy expression of anxiety, and is often triggered by significant fear of a future or current event over which you have no control. The body becomes confused, paralysed with anxiety and starts to shut down in order to remain safe. Panic short-circuits rational thought and directs all energy toward your limbs and body movement to escape a threat.

The family of anxious emotions are important for us to guide our attention. However, overwhelm and panic are seldom useful - although sometimes last minute panic about a looming deadline can inspire us to action! Focus on things you can control, and never let your imagination consume you with thoughts about future events or scenarios out of your control. Reframing anxiety for excitement is a useful way of redirecting energy.

WHAT WILL PEOPLE THINK?
DEADLINES
MEETINGS
TARGETS
PERFORMANCE
BILLS
- MORTGAGE
- ELECTRICITY
- GAS
- FOOD
- INSURANCE
- CAR
- SCHOOL FEES
- INTERNET
- MEDICAL
-1,583.75
EXPENSES
SAVINGS?
- LAUNDRY
- CLEANING
- GROCERIES
- PICK UPS
- MEALS
- REPEAT
MON TUE WED THU FRI SAT SUN
FOOTBALL DANCE TUTOR PRACTICE GAME ? ? ? ?
MUSIC LESSON
PARTY
PARTY
PARENT MEETING
NEVER ENOUGH TIME

# SCARED
*fearful | frightened*

# Summary

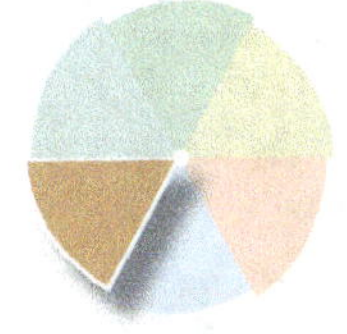

Scared is a very strong fear-based emotion that you feel whenever there is a threat (real or imagined) that you think will put you in danger. This danger could be either physical or psychological pain or harm. You can be scared of things (e.g. spiders, needles, or darkness) or of people who act in ways that trigger hurtful memories or put you in harm's way (e.g. conflict or aggression).

## When does it help?

Have you heard of the fight, flight or freeze response? This is the instinct of what we are likely to do to help us survive when faced with danger. It is fear that helps drive this behaviour. Fear helps us be courageous in the face of danger, but our fears can also be debilitating if we don't control them.

## What happens inside my body?

**large skeletal muscles**
making it easier to flee

**face**
blood drains from face, feeling of blood running cold, playing dead

**adrenaline**
general alert, edgy and ready for action

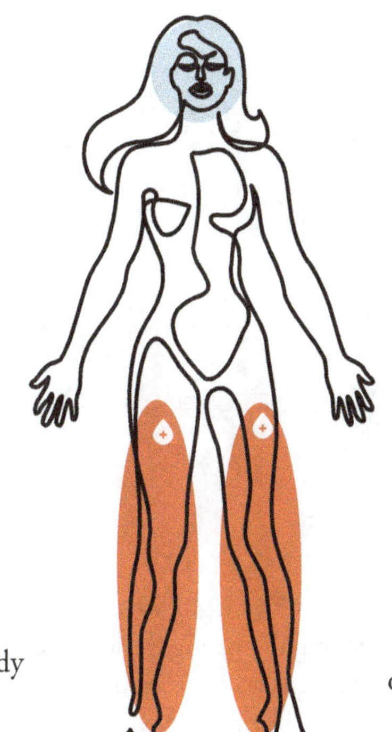


You will be looking for threats, so your eyes and mouth open wide, and your senses seem to all focus on any threat. Your leg muscles get lots of blood ready for movement, and can often start shaking with excess energy if we stay still.

Blood also drains from the face and hands which is a way to signal to predators that we might be dead, causing them to chase others who look more 'alive'. Often people will hide behind their hands to protect their face and vital organs from being attacked.

# Hesitant

*In control, but potential threat noted.*

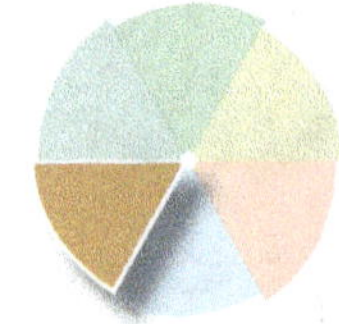

> *"When you're confident, you're going to do things a little differently. You're not going to be hesitant to take a shot, you're not going to be hesitant to make a certain move."*
>
> *- Thich Nhat Hanh*

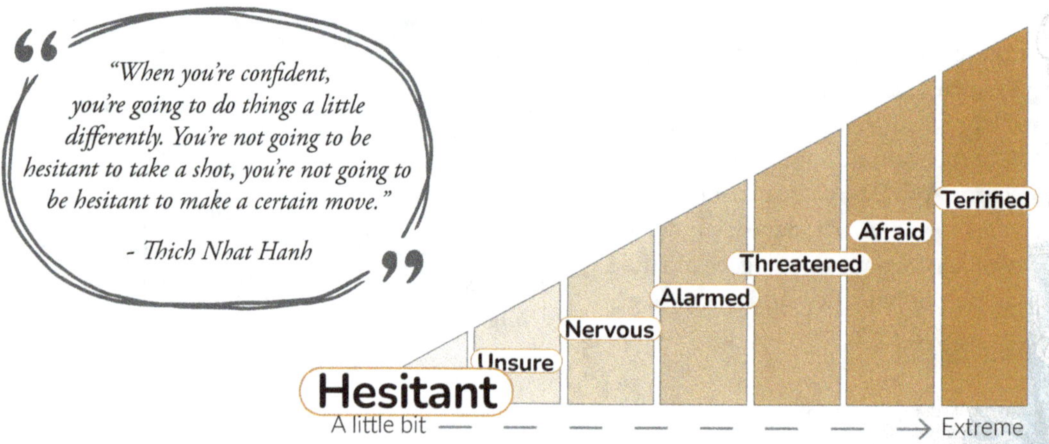


Hesitant is the lightest expression of scared.

Hesitant is often experienced when embarking on a task or journey that is either unknown, new or triggers a negative memory (e.g. he hesitated before asking for more food, not wanting to look greedy). The danger is less obvious than when feeling nervous, but it still causes a moment to stop and think about an action, and weigh up risks and rewards.

Hesitation can also come simply as a result of not knowing what to do, and therefore being scared of doing the wrong thing or making the wrong choice. Good coaches know that creating hesitation or doubt toward an existing behaviour can be the most effective way to break habits and consider alternative options.

# Unsure

*Potential threat identified and being monitored, moving more cautiously.*

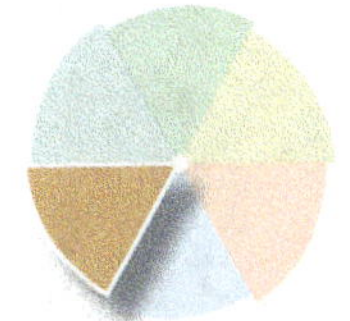

> *"I've been writing songs since I was a teenager, so one kind of song I've written a lot about is, I don't know, teen angst feelings - feeling unsure of yourself and immature."*
>
> *- Ezra Furman*

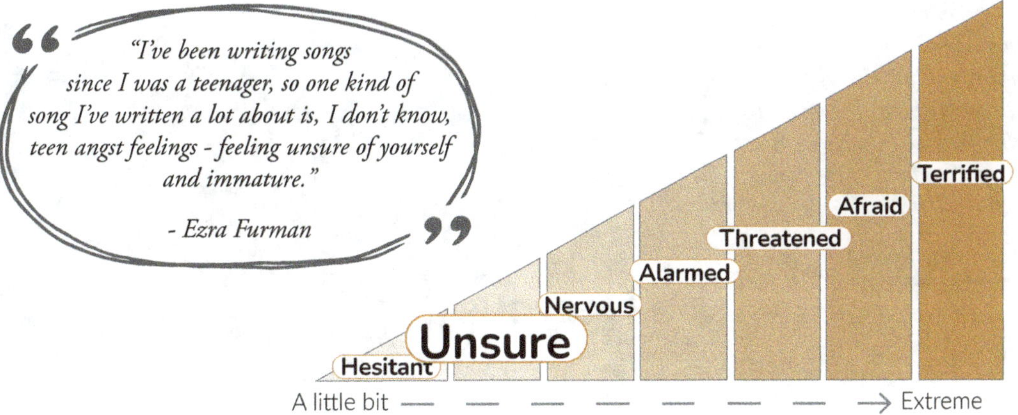


Being unsure is a low level fear, that can be a result of something internal or external.

The fear becomes strong enough to question whether you are in the right place, at the right time, or in the right way. Often being unsure is not related to feeling unsafe, but about a lack of knowing what the right thing to do is.

Being unsure of yourself is a light fear. Most times it is bought on when you don't know the rules of social engagement or acceptable behaviour, for instance the first time you are in someone else's home, when you are new to a class or work environment, or when you meet someone from an unknown cultural background. You don't know if you'll be accepted by their agreed rules, or whether they will abide by your social norms, and this hint of possible of rejection makes us unsure of ourselves, motivating us to increase familiarity and understanding.

# Nervous

*Dangerous situation perceived as likely, movement slow and deliberate.*

> "*I'm not an active person on social media, really. I always get nervous tweeting anything. The moment I tweet, I get this plummeting sense of regret. I delete roughly 95 percent of my tweets immediately.*"
>
> *- Charlotte Ritchie*

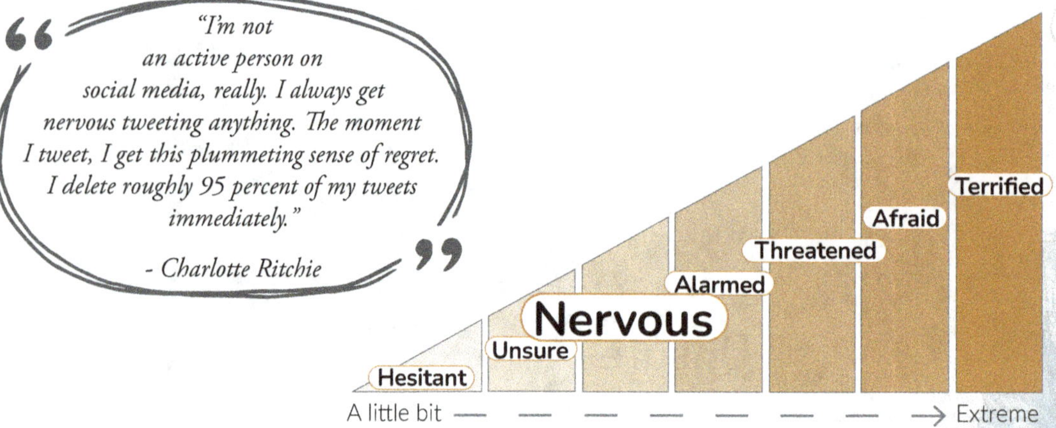


Most of us are nervous when presented with new or novel situations.

People also experience nervousness where the potential of a negative outcome is real, even if you have the confidence that success is probable. It is a stress response, producing the hormone adrenaline to help deal with a perceived or imagined threat, which can feel like 'butterflies' in your stomach.

Nervousness is normal, and can be helpful. Ultimately, new challenges and opportunities help us grow. Nervousness is your natural preparation system for something outside your comfort zone. Accepting that it's a completely natural experience, and reframing nerves as anticipation can help keep things in check and in control.

# Alarmed

*The tipping point of conscious thought being overtaken by unconscious reactions.*

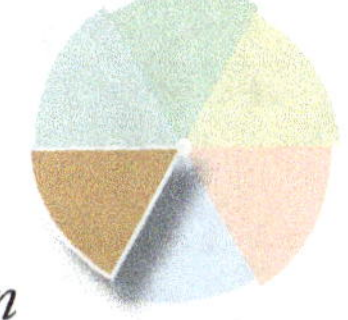

*"Before we are alarmed, we see correctly; when we are alarmed, we see double; and when we have been alarmed, we see nothing but trouble."*

*- The Count of Monte Cristo, Alexandre Dumas,*

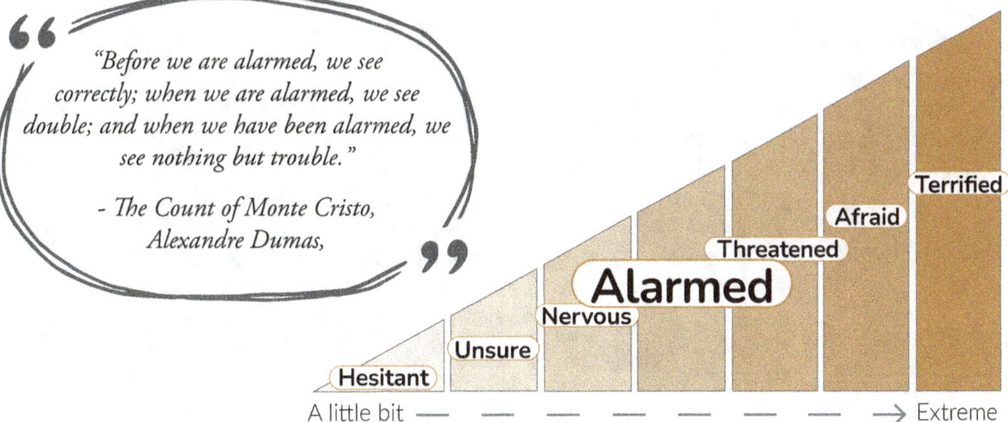


Alarmed is the gateway between the something being perceived as potentially dangerous, to most likely being dangerous.

Being alarmed puts your emotional reactivity on notice, and you are on the edge of allowing your reactive brain to take over in order to get yourself somewhere safe. Alarmed takes a fair amount of energy, so is unhealthy to sustain for long periods.

When fear reaches this level your internal 'alarm' system starts to ring. This can be very good when we want to do activities like cross the road safely, or make sure we don't accidentally walk near a dangerous animal. Escaping the feeling of being alarmed safely can even be entertaining, with many people enjoying scary movies or stories that are alarming. Rarely do we enjoy things that tip us into states of fear higher than this, which can trigger traumatic memories and a genuine fear of being unsafe.

# Threatened

*Losing control and rational thought - often very reactive and lashing out.*

> *"One ought never to turn one's back on a threatened danger and try to run away from it. If you do that, you will double the danger. But if you meet it promptly and without flinching, you will reduce the danger by half."*
>
> *- Winston Churchill*

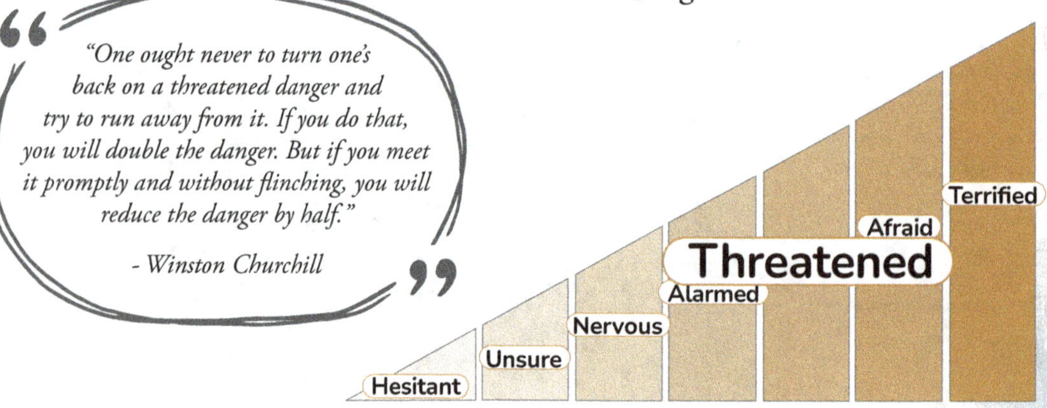


Threatened is a strong expression of scared, and usually triggered when your psychological or physical safety is under threat.

While the natural reaction to feeling afraid or terrified is to hide or run away, people tend to lash out when feeling threatened. People take a defensive posture, and express aggression on their face similar to anger (preparing to defend themselves).

In order to survive for as long as we humans have, our brain routinely tricks us into making two mistakes: overestimating threats and underestimating opportunities. This has been a great way to survive, but not so great for thriving in the modern age.

# Afraid

*Lost control, irrational behaviour.*

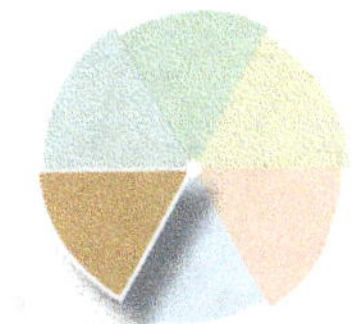

> "I learnt that courage was not the absence of fear, but the triumph over it. The brave man is not he who does not feel afraid, but he who conquers that fear."
>
> - Nelson Mandela

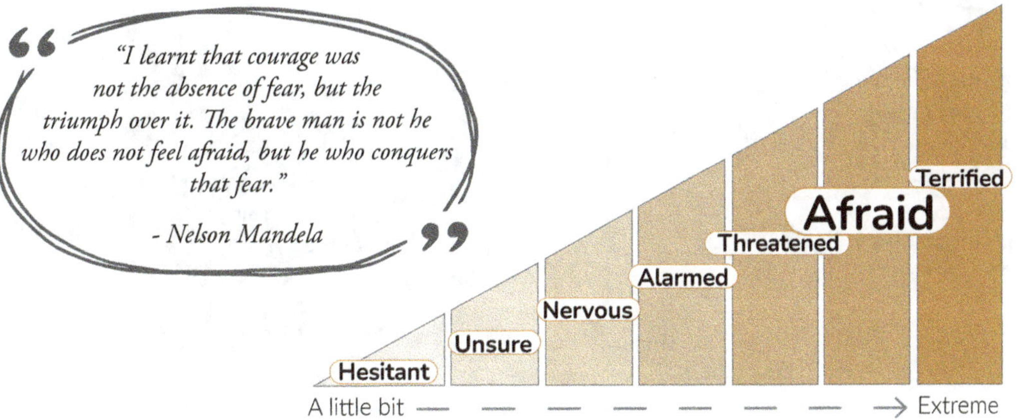


Being afraid is an extremely strong and debilitating emotion.

It is often expressed immediately prior to an activity or incident where the likelihood of a painful outcome is seen as extremely likely. Being brave is when people put aside this emotion and their own safety to help themselves or someone else avoid danger. When feeling afraid, legs tend to shake, arms and hands can feel clammy and cold, and eyes remain wide open.

Feelings of being afraid can help keep you be attentive to danger and risk when needing to be courageous. Controlling fear in this state usually consists of slowing down breathing, talking positively to yourself, and knowing when to remove yourself from danger. Being scared for a long period of time is exhausting. When afraid you're not acting rationally, but running on instinct.

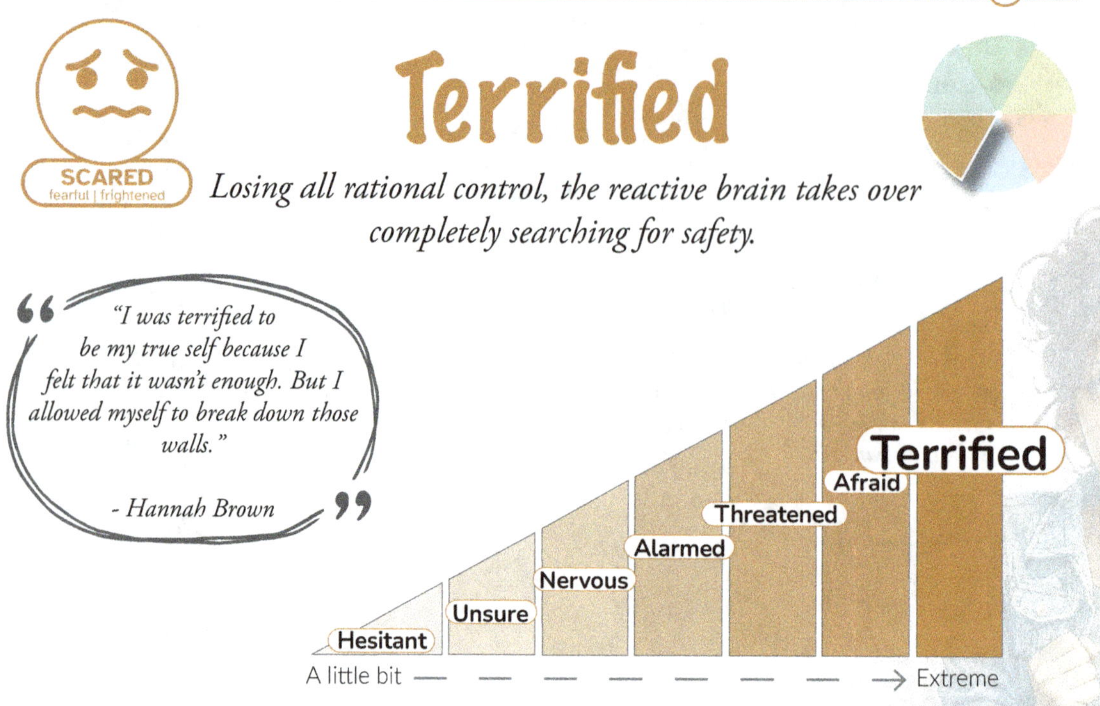


# Terrified

*Losing all rational control, the reactive brain takes over completely searching for safety.*

> *"I was terrified to be my true self because I felt that it wasn't enough. But I allowed myself to break down those walls."*
>
> *- Hannah Brown*

Terrified is the strongest scared emotion.

It describes an intense emotional state where fear becomes completely overwhelming. Usually causing people to run away or crouch in a fetal position to protect themselves from what they fear. Being terrified is crippling, and people who live a lot in this state of fear become extremely antisocial and unhealthy.

You can't overcome a terrifying fear that remains in your subconscious. You must face it. Make the implicit, explicit. If you are in a safe place, turn toward your fear (not away from it), and curiously explore it. Awareness of the what and why something scares you helps overcome it. As always, make sure you are in a safe place — facing the things that terrify you doesn't mean putting yourself in harm's way or intentionally being around dangerous people.

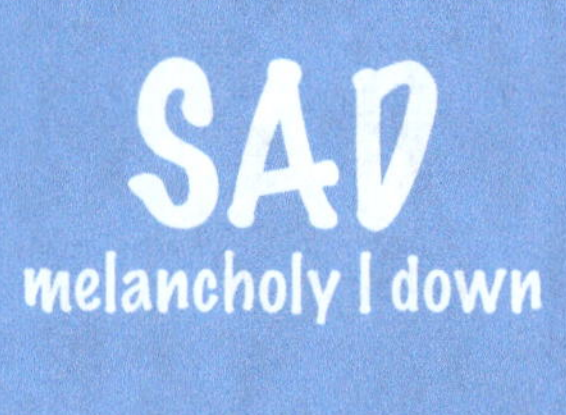
SAD
melancholy | down

HAPPY
motivated | energised

We call this the wholeness dimension because it's where different emotions come together to give us a sense of completeness. These aren't opposites. They're more like colours that can exist at the same time, blending to show how you're really experiencing life. It's entirely possible to feel grief and peace together, or to be discouraged and still quietly optimistic.

Sadness, at its core, is the brain's response to loss. The skill isn't to remove it, but to work with it. When we can experience lower-intensity sadness, like disappointment, while also holding steadier emotions like calm or peace, we navigate life far more effectively.

At a deeper level, this balance between sadness and happiness is really about hope. Whether we feel hopeful or hopeless. You can feel sad and still believe things will improve. Or you can feel relatively fine on the surface but quietly carry a sense that nothing will get better.

Emotional agency is about managing that balance. Not eliminating difficult emotions, but allowing them to sit alongside more grounded ones, so they inform us without overwhelming us, and so hope remains available, even in hard moments.

# HAPPY
motivated | energised

**HAPPY**
joyful | Optimistic

# Summary

Happiness is the emotion we all like the most. It indicates we are calm and safe, which then allows us to feel things like love and connectedness. Happiness is not an emotion we can, or should, always be in, but finding ways to induce happiness can be very useful. Laughing for no reason can be a great way to inspire happiness in yourself and those around you.

## When does it help?

Happiness is the body's way of regulating other strong emotions. This is why people often laugh after they've been scared at a sudden loud noise. Happiness also mitigates for extreme anxiety or sadness, but be careful - sometimes we need to feel the other emotions, and trying to make others happy when they are sad, anxious or angry can be uncaring and unempathetic.

## What happens inside my body?

### Chemical inhibitors

Neurally inhibiting negative or anxious thoughts

### Dopamine

The 'happy' drug - recovery mechanism from heightened arousal (think of laughing after being scared, or escaping danger)

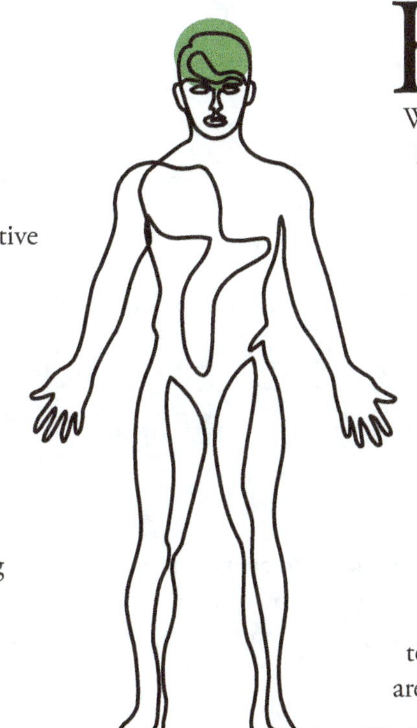

Happiness is largely a reaction that happens in the brain and face. When happy, you can smile or laugh, and when mixed with a little excitement, can also result in clapping. You might see this after an amazing performance where people will stand, cheer and clap. Happiness produces an overall sense of lightness and peace, and can release **dopamine** in your brain to reinforce that something is good. When you are happy, all your worries seem to fade away, due to the chemical inhibitors that are also released.

# Peaceful

*In control, conscious, completely comfortable, and without agitation.*

> *"Just as treasures are uncovered from the earth, so virtue appears from good deeds, and wisdom appears from a pure and peaceful mind."*
>
> *- Buddah*

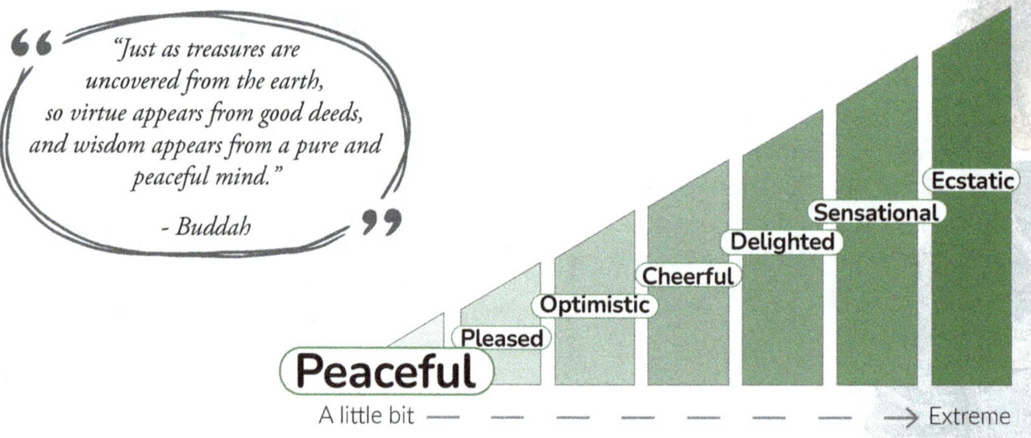


The most restful form of happiness, peaceful, is the state that allows us the most control over our thoughts and actions.

In a peaceful state, the brain is feeling safe, secure, confident and content with the present moment. When peaceful, all the muscles in the forehead and jaw relax, a soft smile emerges, and eyes are not fully open (there is no need to take in all environmental information).

This state is also the one experienced when people are working on something they love doing, simply because they want to do it (not because of an impending deadline or external expectations). When feeling peaceful, time can seem to fly past, as our internal time monitoring system is less active.

# Pleased

*In control, joy from an unexpected outcome.*

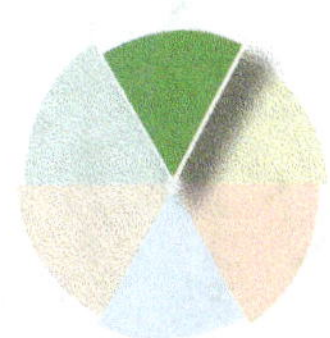

"*I am pleased, with a feeling of good fortune, to be from Selanik. If you want to know the truth better, I feel that my chest is overflowing with a feeling of pride.*"

*- Mustafa Kemal Ataturk*

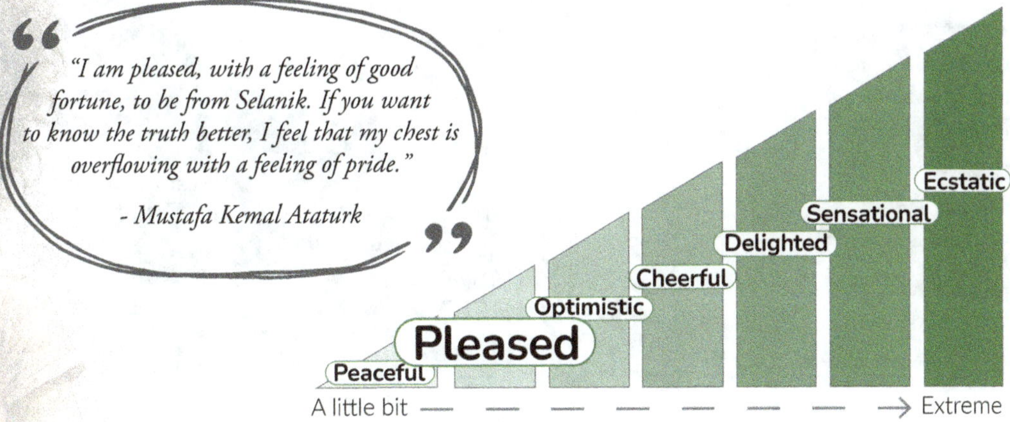


Pleased sits between the very low arousal of peaceful, and the slightly more intense happiness of optimistic.

When we are pleased it is usually a level of happiness with a nice situation or a favourable outcome. The results haven't necessarily exceeded your expectations, but you are pleased with the result. In this way, it is possible pleased can often be tinged with a hint of disappointment.

Pleased to meet you. Pleased to have achieved what we have achieved. Pleased that we are feeling better. When we are pleased we hold a small sense of hopefulness, and feel good about what we have achieved, or the situation we find ourselves in. The brain isn't necessarily pumping dopamine (the feel good drug) into our system, but we are aware that things could be worse. In this way being pleased is akin to being grateful or thankful.

# Optimistic

*In control, motivated, and positive about the future.*

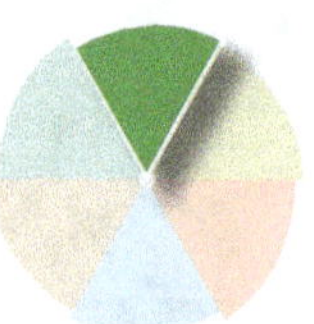



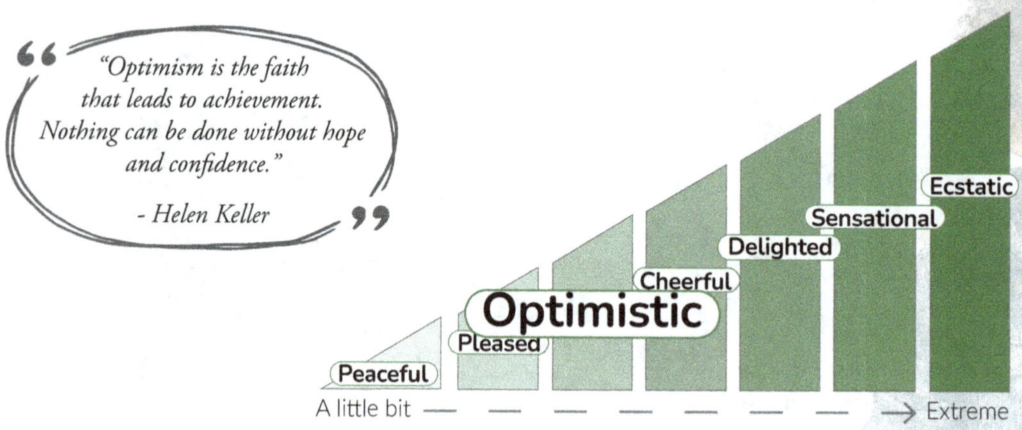



A slightly more energetic form of happiness than pleased, optimism is hope and positive expectations of future events.

When optimistic, people will often speak up more in group settings, and feel eager to 'get stuck into things' so they can reach the future state quicker and maximise the positive outcomes. Optimism can turn into irritation or frustration if someone seems to be undermining action with unrealistic negativity or worry.

Moving between optimistic, cheerful and peaceful is often an effective way to navigate many life situations where proactive energy is needed. Learning to find these emotional states and resist the temptation to move into an aggressive or fear emotion, helps us keep in control and be less reactive.

# Cheerful

*Relaxed and less controlled, lots of smiling.*

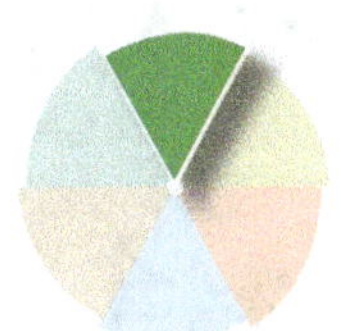

> *"Wondrous is the strength of cheerfulness, and its power of endurance - the cheerful person will do more in the same time, will do it; better, will preserve it longer, than the sad or sullen."*
>
> *- Thomas Carlyle*

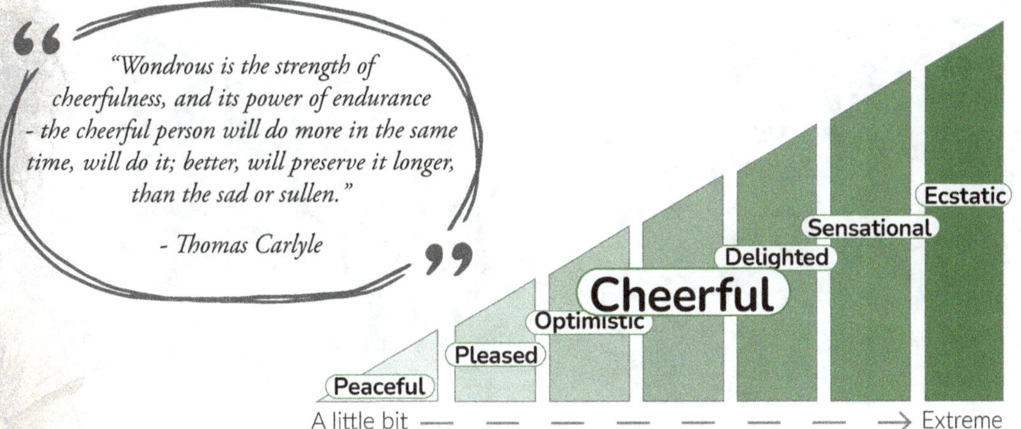



As humans we love to win, and cheerful is the emotion we feel when we are winning.

Cheerful has more energy than optimistic, but is still in control of thoughts and actions (that can be lost in delighted and sensational). Medium levels of dopamine (the brain's feel-good drug) are released when cheerful, resulting in a big smile and often some body movement to release energy (like clapping or thrusting fists in the air).

Cheerful, sensational and ecstatic are all emotions that are hard to maintain over a long period of time. Learning to experience these states for a time and then consciously dialling it back to an optimistic or peaceful state can be the key to feeling content and remaining within the family of happy emotions. Be careful not to use them to simply suppress other emotions. Remember, all emotions have their time and place.

# Delighted

*Higher energy state that is less conscious of immediate surroundings.*

"*I have always been delighted at the prospect of a new day, a fresh try, one more start, with perhaps a bit of magic waiting somewhere behind the morning.*"

*- J. B. Priestley*

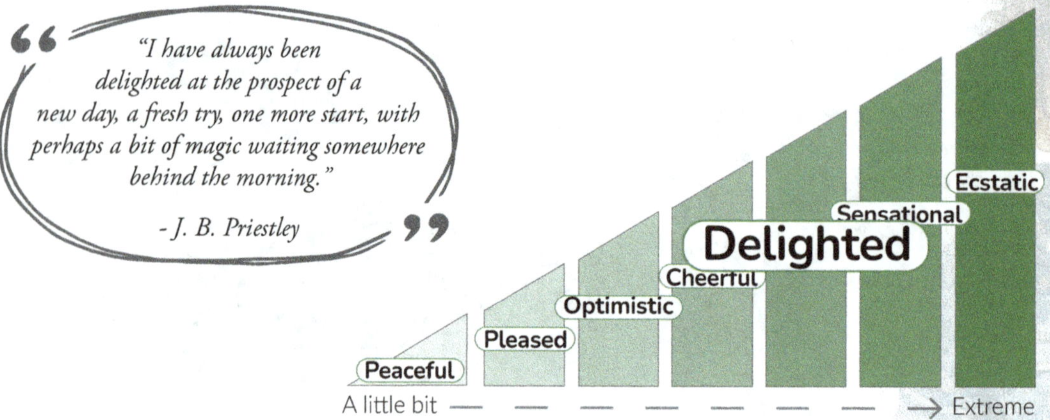


The expression of delight is often mixed with a level of excitement and we are not always in control of our actions.

When we are delighted to meet someone we often become unaware of others in a conversation, with our attention firmly fixed on the person we are delighted to meet. We are delighted when something unexpectedly good happens, or we meet someone we admire.

When we are delighted our brain releases serotonin and dopamine, two chemicals that make us feel good and immediately enhance our mood. The excitement that often accompanies delight causes our eyes to widen and our movements more pronounced (like shaking hands more vigorously, nodding, or having a slight 'skip' in our step).

# Sensational

*Little control or awareness of surroundings.*

> *"The bride's family created a fresh, radiant and stunning reception that left the bridal party and all the wedding guests feeling sensational on the wedding day."*
>
> *- Paula Gallum*

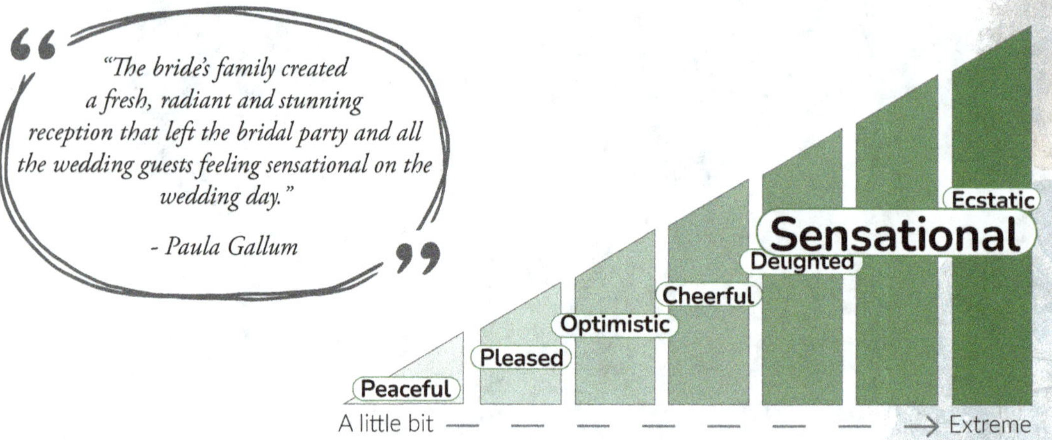


Sensational is sometimes referred to as being in a 'blindly optimistic' state.

It is often experienced with an unexpected win, or at the beginning of something new and exciting (e.g falling in love). It can also be triggered by large groups applauding or recognising your achievements. It is a high energy state that can be exhausting after some time, which can lead to sadness while you recover mental energy and realign to reality.

It can be difficult to see the more extreme expressions of happiness as undesirable, but long bouts of sensationalism or ecstatic euphoria 'overcooks' the brain's reward system and triggers the brain into a more depressed recovery mode.

# Ecstatic

*Little to no consciousness of people or things in your immediate environment.*

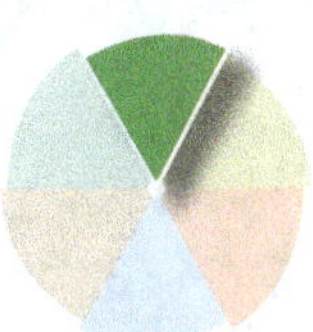

> *"I was ecstatic when we won - to host the Olympics is one of the biggest opportunities in living memory."*
>
> *- Sebastian Coe*

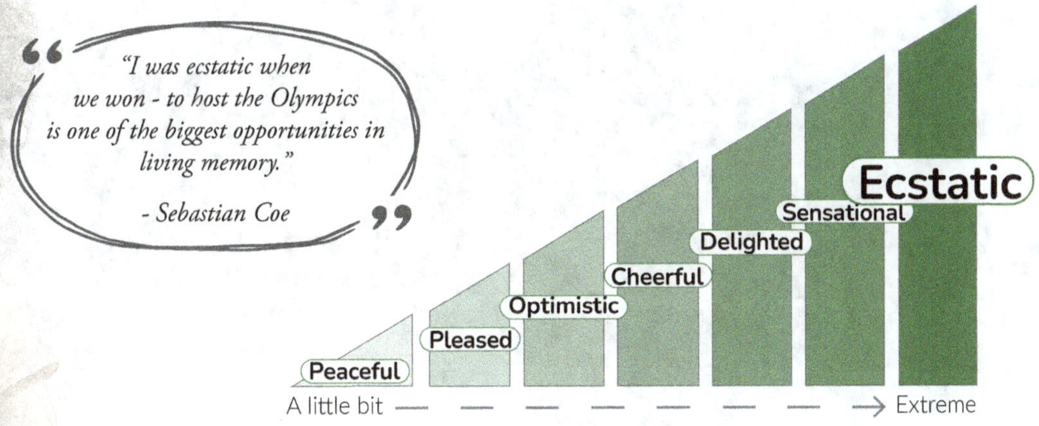


Ecstatic is an extreme expression of happiness.

Most often reserved for events in life that are positive, unexpected, or that you have been looking forward to for a long time (like seeing your favourite performer on stage). Ecstatic is an extremely high energy emotional state, and people can feel depressed when coming down from a significant, ecstatic emotional state.

When you are ecstatic you are definitely not in control of your behaviours and actions. For some, fainting can be the result of being overly ecstatic, overwhelmed with the situation at hand, triggering a deep 'sleep' mode to recover. Enjoy moments of extreme happiness, but don't stay there too long or work yourself into a frenzied state (where you may not remember much).

# SAD
### melancholy | down

# Summary

Sadness is often explained as the opposite of happiness. It is a feeling of sorrow and usually makes us want to be by ourselves or with people we know really well. Sadness is usually a result of loss, grief, change, disappointment or a feeling of helplessness (when it seems like you are unable to avoid a future negative outcome or event).

## When does it help?

We need periods of sadness for our brain to recover from losing something that we had, or thought we would have in the future. At a higher intensity level this includes the grieving process - our brain's way of healing the mental trauma caused by unexpected loss events. Try not to totally isolate yourself when sad - stay connected to loved ones.

## What happens inside my body?

Chemicals slow metabolism and turn attention inward to help recover from loss

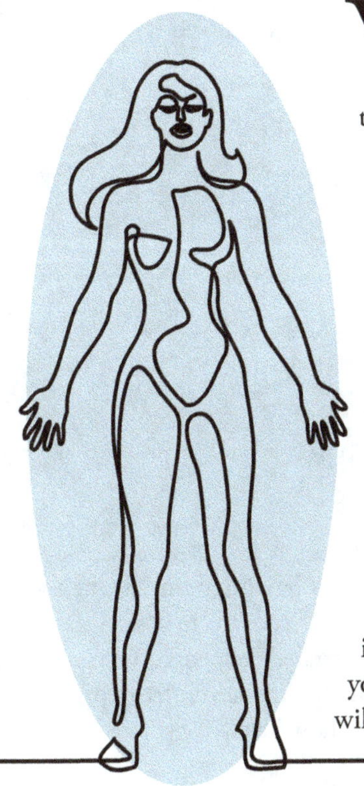

When you are sad you can feel 'heavy', low in energy and not inclined to talk a lot with others. Often this means you want to lie down and sleep a lot. Sometimes your body will want to cry, which is what it does when it needs to relieve pain. You may not feel like eating much, and all the muscles in your face that you use to smile will relax. Your thoughts also tend to slow down and motivation levels seem to fade away. It's okay to go there, just don't stay there. Take the time you need, but let other people in who can share the journey with you—even if you don't feel like it, it will be helpful.

# Disappointed

*In control, but feel a slight heaviness.*

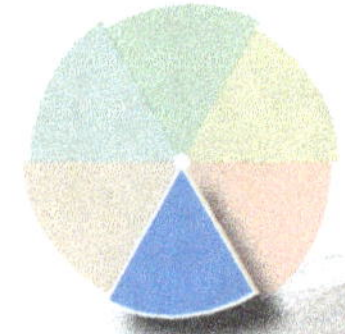

> *"For some time, I thought Apollo 13 was a failure. I was disappointed I didn't get to land on the moon. But actually, it turned out to be the best thing that could have happened."*
>
> *- Jim Lovell*

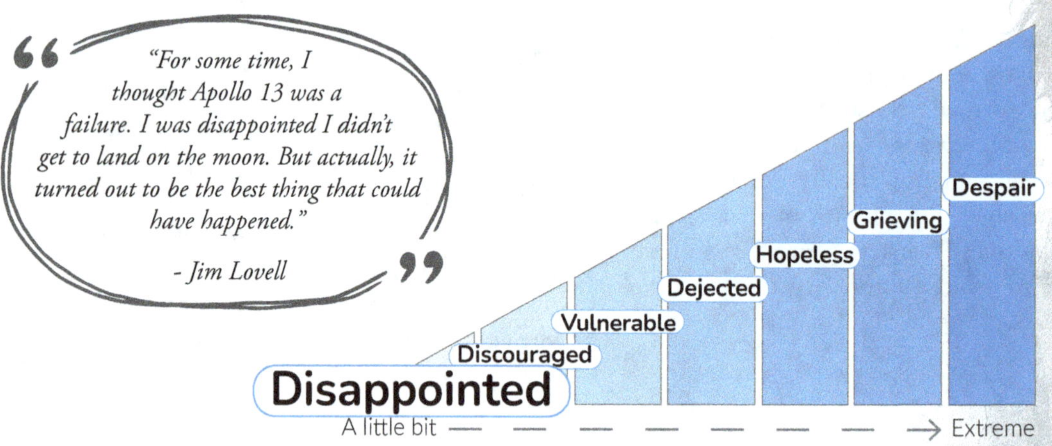


Disappointment is a mild sadness, and often felt when faced with unrealised expectations in yourself or others.

"I am disappointed that it didn't go as well as I hoped." When disappointed people often close their eyes or look down to help shut out the world for a bit and allow attention to be directed internally. Disappointment is also often felt when someone's self-worth is being questioned, or they feel embarrassed.

It can be necessary to allow yourself to be disappointed when you need to. Allowing yourself to be openly disappointed can indicate you are in a safe place, and simply in need of some time and space. Try not to get frustrated at people who crowd your space when you feel disappointed in yourself as this will only make you feel worse. Just realise they are usually just concerned about you and trying to show love.

# Discouraged

*Still in control, but motivation takes a hit.*

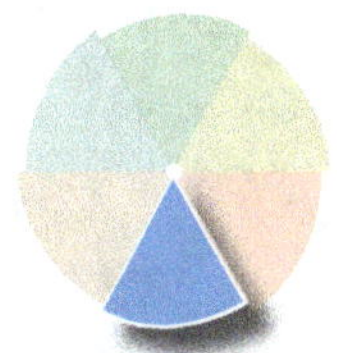



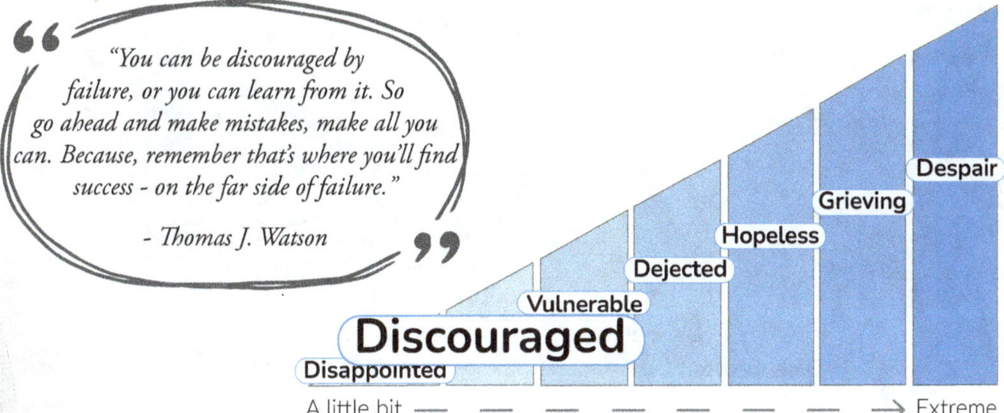


Discouragement is an expression of sadness that helps us recover from failure, pain, hurtful words, or unrealised dreams or expectations.

Drooping eyelids, downcast eyes, lowered lip corners, and slanting inner eyebrows all indicate discouragement and hopelessness, with the facial expressions of hopelessness more pronounced.

Discouragement is often a temporary emotion that can be alleviated by an encouraging word, or moment of humour, that helps reframe our circumstance and re-insert confidence and self-belief. This is different from more intense sad emotions (hopeless, grief or despair), where this approach can be seen as unempathetic).

# Vulnerable

*Still in control, but we still suffering the pain of loss.*

> *"We're never so vulnerable than when we trust someone - but paradoxically, if we cannot trust, neither can we find love or joy."*
>
> *- Walter Anderson*

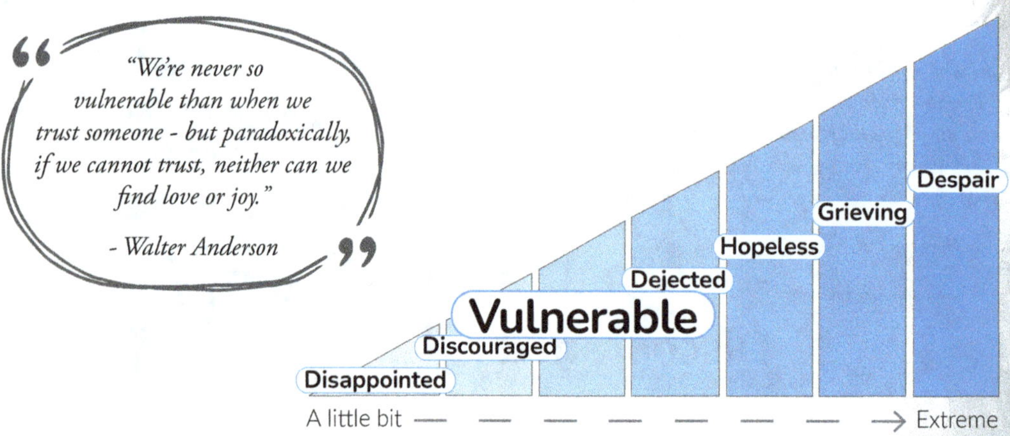



Between discouraged and dejected we reach a state of vulnerability.

This is the shaky ground that you reach if the loss you are experiencing is related to self-assuredness, big enough to have an impact on your daily life, and results in you not feeling as secure as you did before.

Vulnerability is triggered when we lose something that has previously provided safety. This could be realising we are not as competent as we thought we were, or someone who helped us feel safe is no longer available to us. Vulnerability is often coupled with anxiety, and the present feeling of vulnerability quickly triggers a worry for what might happen in the future. Separation anxiety is often treated by establishing safe spaces and relationships that make people less vulnerable in the present, and therefore not longer worried about their future safety.

# Dejected

*On the edge of losing motivation and control.*

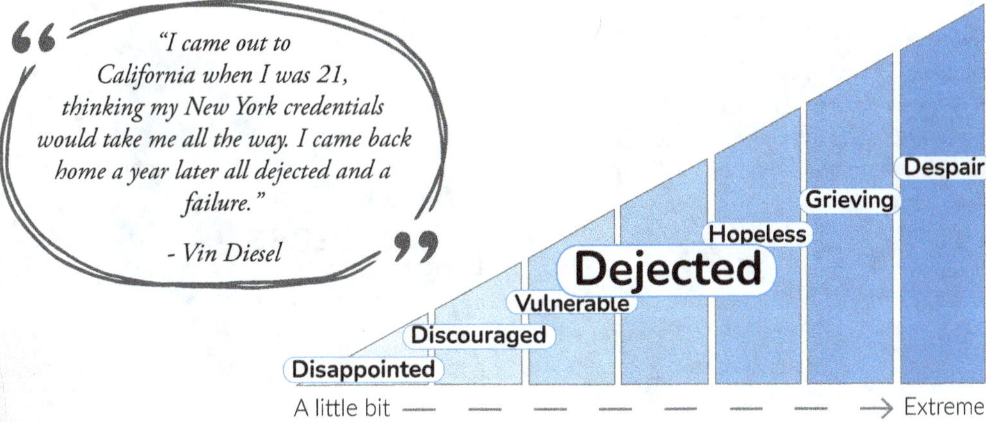


We feel dejected when we fall short of our own expectations, or realise that something we hoped for will not be a reality.

This is not as strong as hopeless, and is usually directed toward a specific event, situation or relationship. If left unchecked, or if the cause is assumed to be something out of our control, it can escallate to a more pervasive sense of hopelessness.

At the point of dejectedness in the sadness scale we see increased activity in different parts of the brain such as the thalamus, the amygdala, and the hippocampus - all parts of our unconscious brain. The hippocampus in particular is strongly linked with memory, and it makes sense that these highly sad responses are imprinting an awareness of certain memories in our brain to warn us in the future. When we feel dejected we are on the edge of slipping into a state of depression.

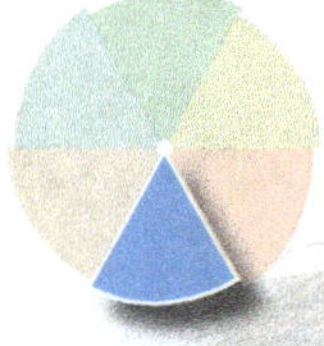

# Hopeless

*Losing control, with negative thoughts depressing the mood significantly.*

> *"Youth is the period in which you can be hopeless. The end of every episode is the end of the world. But the power of hoping through everything, the knowledge that the soul survives its adventures, that great inspiration comes with age."*
>
> *- Gilbert K. Chesterton*

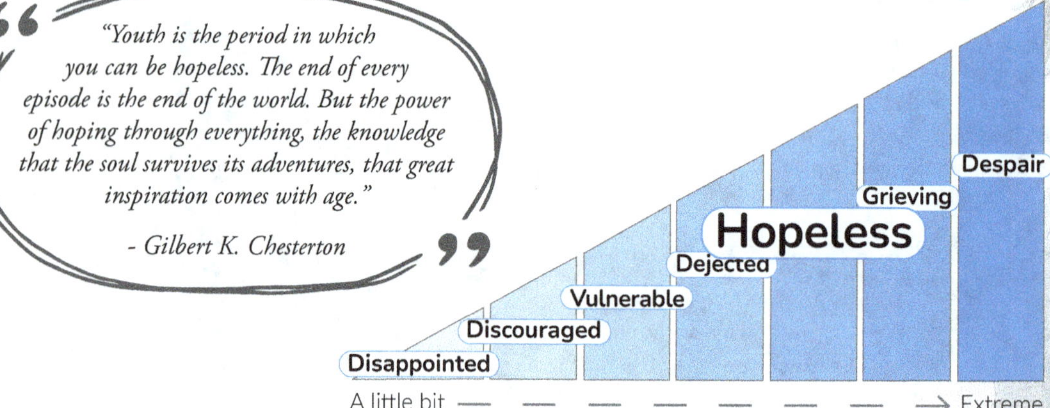


Hopelessness is a higher energy expression of sadness.

Usually reserved for times where we feel powerless and worthless, or it can be felt following other high emotional states, such as ecstasy, panic or terror. Sometimes people cry as a way of releasing energy and processing memories and emotion. Often there is a need to be close to others, without the need to talk or engage. Being connected and safe is enough.

Feeling hopeless without reason or explanation can often move you to grief or anguish as you don't know how you got into the state, and therefore don't know how to get out of it. Time and patience is often all that is needed to move out of this state, but spending too much time there can lead to the more intense expressions of grieving and despair.

# Grieving

*We need time to heal from loss, we have little rational control.*

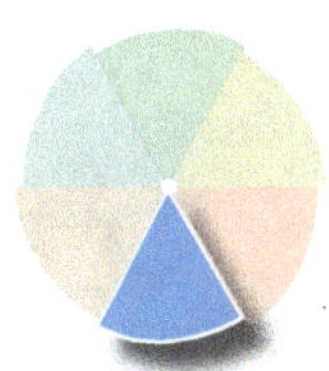

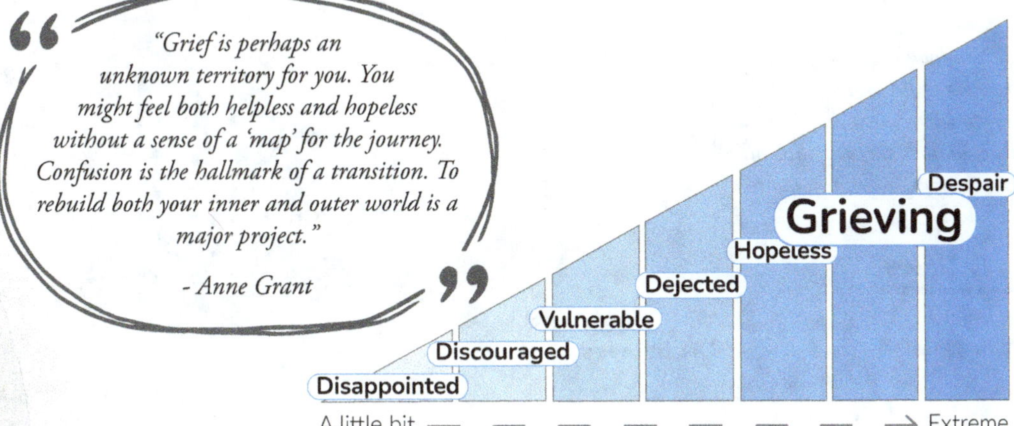


> *"Grief is perhaps an unknown territory for you. You might feel both helpless and hopeless without a sense of a 'map' for the journey. Confusion is the hallmark of a transition. To rebuild both your inner and outer world is a major project."*
>
> *- Anne Grant*

Grieving is often the result of significant change or loss of someone or something important to you, or something you've become accustomed to.

Often people who are experiencing grief will want to isolate from social contact, and keep themselves in dark, comfortable places to help focus and privately process their thoughts and situation. People can also have unexpected bursts of crying, which can be a cathartic release of built up energy.

The seven stages of grieving are shock & denial, pain & self-loathing, anger & bargaining, depression & isolation, turning a corner, reconstructing the future, and hope & acceptance. Going through this grieving process is healthy, and necessary in relevant circumstances, but extended periods of grieving can actually lead to emotional trauma and periods of deep depression. Knowing how to sense when you need to move through the different stages can be the key to mental resilience and finding hope.

# Despair

*The mind has shut down, consumed by irrational thoughts.*

> *"If you look for truth, you may find comfort in the end; if you look for comfort you will not get either comfort or truth only soft soap and wishful thinking to begin, and in the end, despair."*
>
> *- C. S. Lewis*

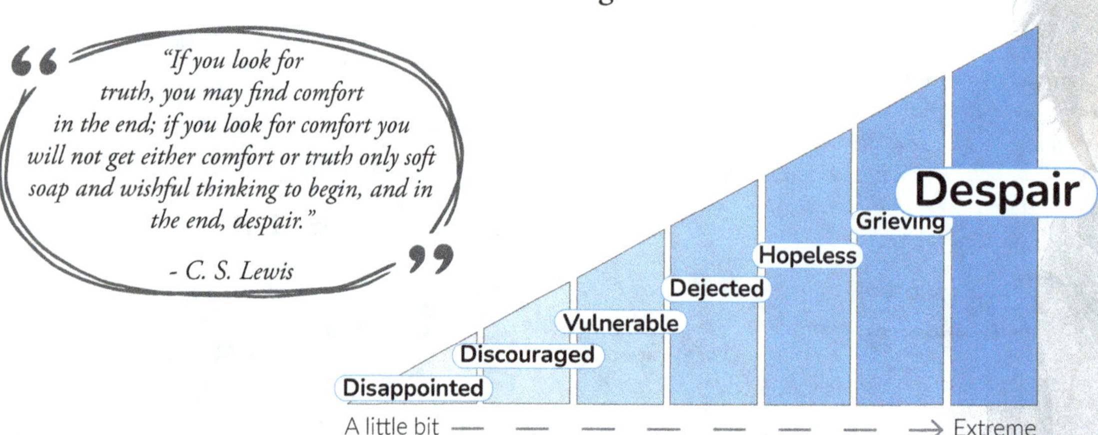


Despair is a state where the mind and body are so activated by sadness that your brain shuts down.

It is often triggered by extended periods of hopelessness or grief. Being in a state of despair causes physical changes in the brain, overwhelming entire thought processes and motivating people to isolate and sleep.

The persistent expression of extreme sadness, or loss of interest that characterises anguish, can lead to a range of symptoms including dramatic changes in sleep patterns, appetite, general energy levels, concentration, daily routines and self-esteem. Unlike grieving, even if you can sense when you need to move out of despair, it can sometimes feel impossible to do. Like you are lost in the dark and can't find the light switch. If you think you are experiencing long periods of despair, it's a good idea to seek help. There are many ways to escape the pain of despair that lead to a hopeful and happy life, even if you can't see any in the moment. Sometimes we just need some help to find the light switch.

# SURPRISE

# DISGUST

Two extra emotions that aren't in the Switch Emotion Wheel™, but worthy of mentioning...

# Surprise & Disgust

Surprise is an often overlooked emotion as it is one of the briefest emotions that we feel. It arises when we encounter sudden and unexpected sounds or movements. Its function is to focus our attention on what is happening and quickly assess if it is dangerous or not.

Disgust is a core survival emotion that makes us want to expel something toxic to us. We can feel disgusted by something we perceive with our physical senses (sight, smell, touch, sound, taste), by the actions or appearances of others, and even by ideas.

## What happens inside my body?

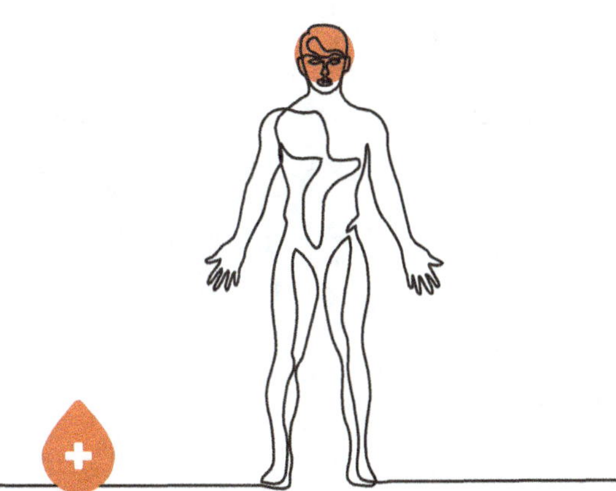

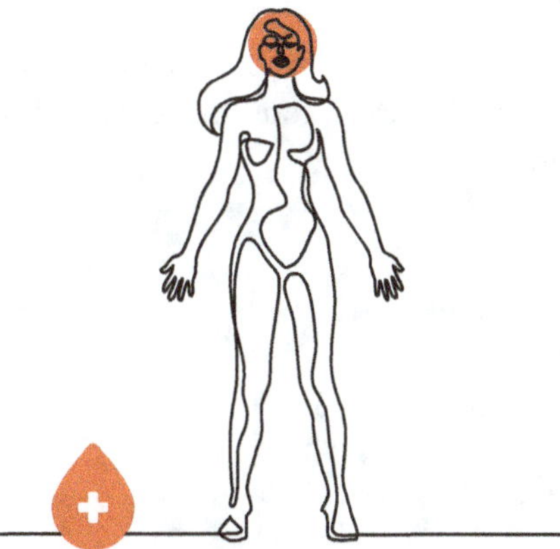

### Eyebrows, face

Eyes open wide to allow more light on the retina to increase visual information

### Nose, lips

Upper lip curls ready to spit out poison. Nostrils close to reject a noxious odour. Frown to disapprove

## Why are they not on the Switch Emotion Wheel?

While these are really useful emotions, they are only felt momentarily and are a natural reaction to the environment. Therefore they are unlikely to need to be understood and managed in the same way as the emotions represented on the Switch Emotion Wheel™ that have a much larger impact on our day to day activities and interpersonal connections.

# Is Tiredness An Emotion?

*sometimes I simply feel exhausted...*

No, tiredness is not an emotion. You do FEEL tired, but it's important to separate tiredness from emotion. Tiredness is an amplifier of emotion. When you are exhausted you have less energy to inhibit or manage the intensity of your emotions. The more tired you are, the more likely you are to bounce between more extreme emotions. Sleep is a really, really good thing when it comes to managing your emotions. But it is not an emotion.

# A Final Word

Emotions are extraordinary things. They are not problems to be solved, but signals to be understood and energy to be used. When we learn to work with them, rather than against them, we become better humans and far more effective at life.

If this Little Book of Big Emotions has shifted even a small part of how you think, notice, or respond, then it has done its job. The real value, though, is not in reading it.

It's in using it.

In the quiet moments. In the difficult conversations. In the split second where you could react, but choose something better.

And if it has been useful, don't keep it to yourself. Pass it on. Share the ideas. Start the conversations. Because emotional agency is not just a personal advantage, it's a collective one.

The more people who understand how to use emotion well, the better our schools, workplaces, families, and communities become.

Thank you for taking the time to read, to reflect, and to stay curious.

That, more than anything, is where this work begins.

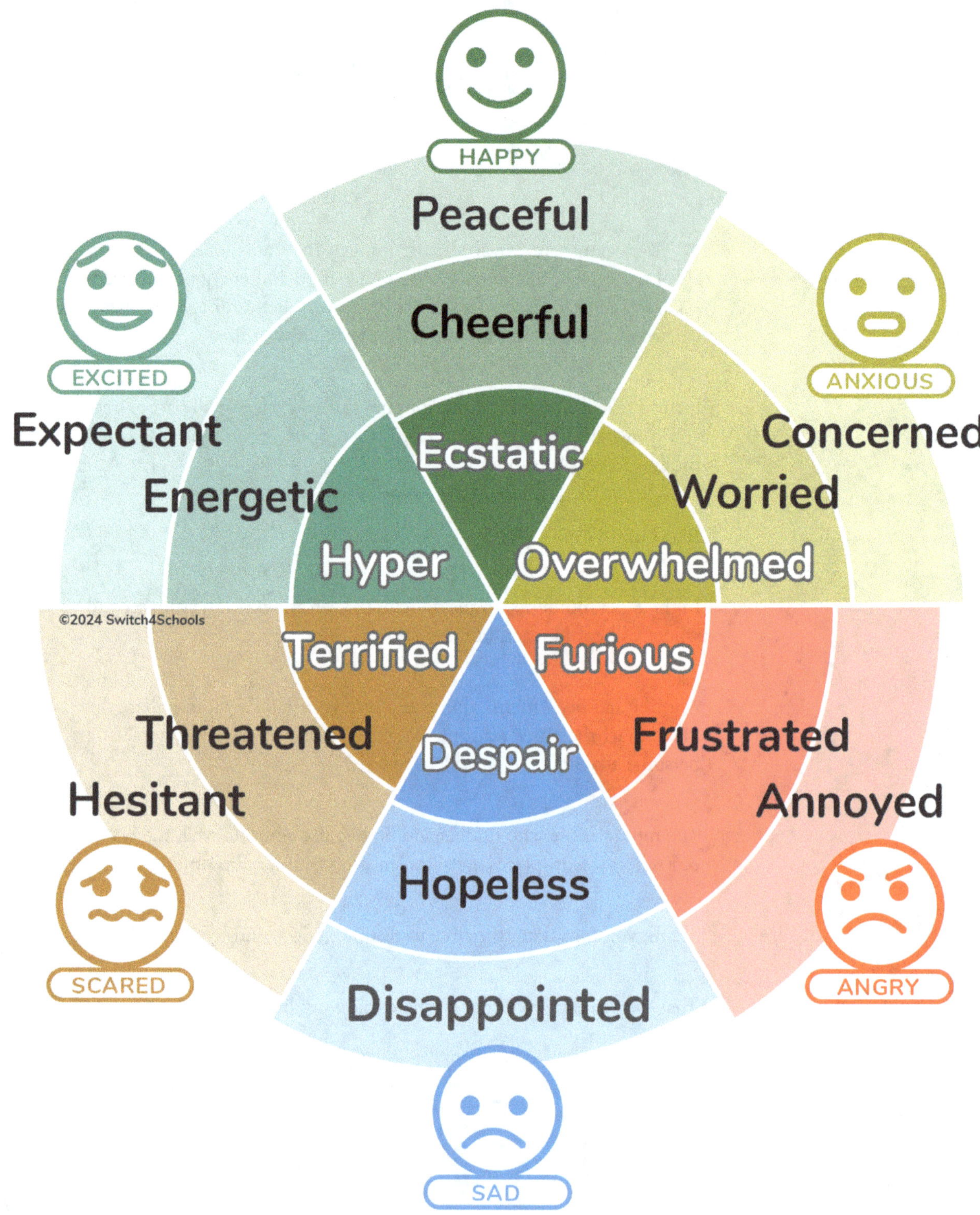


The Switch 3-level Emotion Wheel™

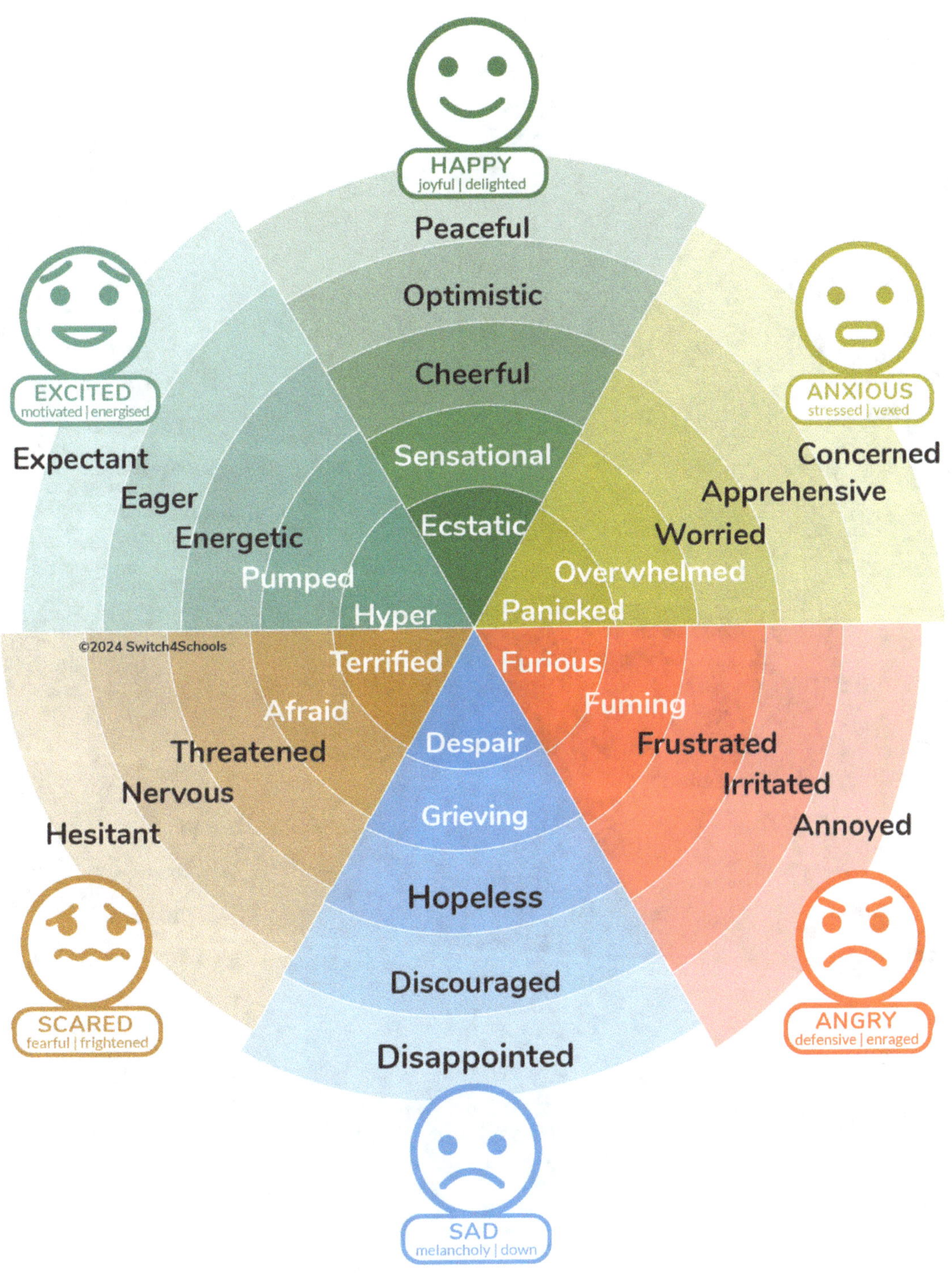


The Switch 5-level Emotion Wheel™®

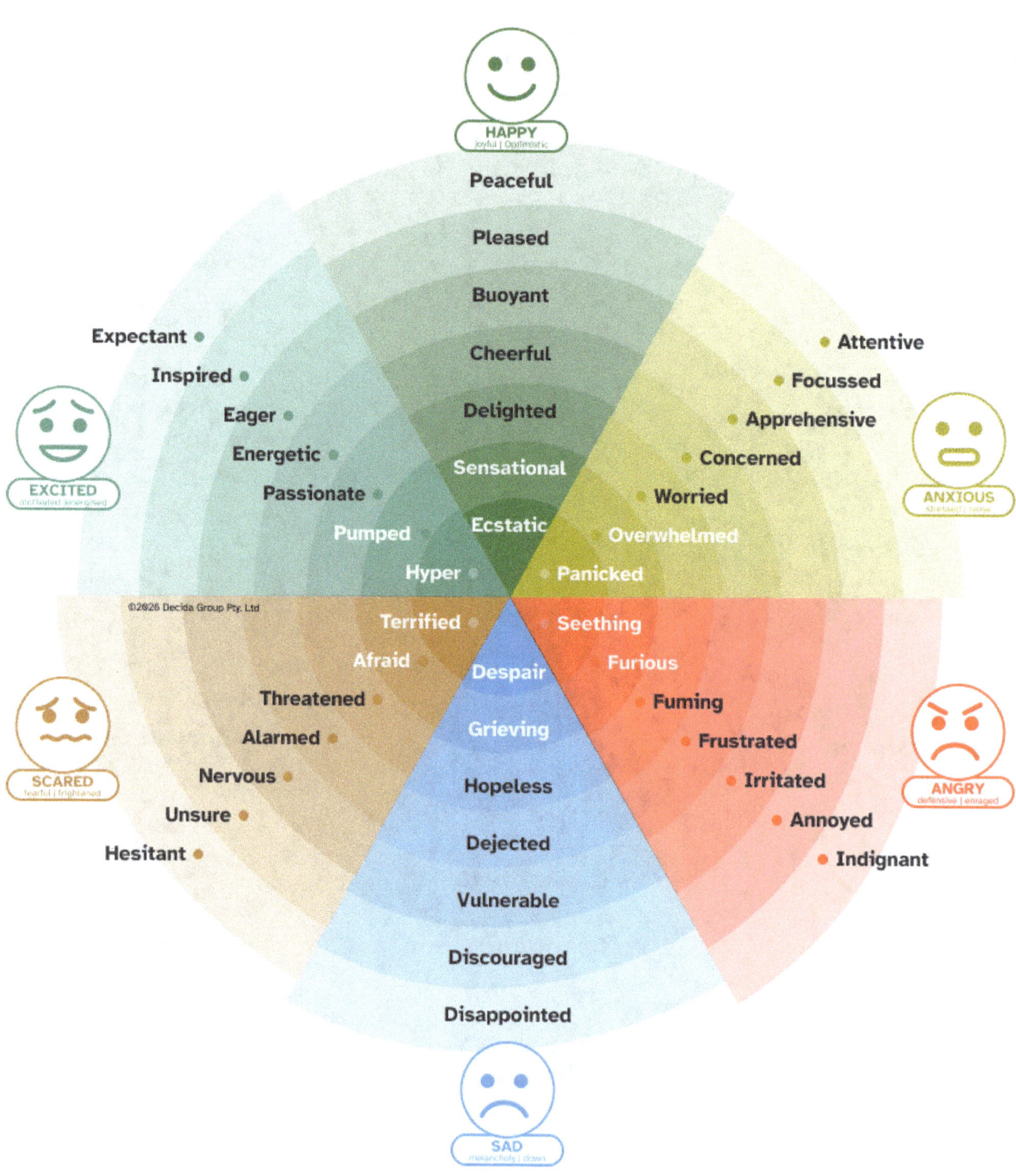


The Switch 7-level Emotion Wheel™®

Switch4Schools is a research-based, award-winning, turn-key digital platform. It builds emotional agency, monitors wellbeing, builds culture, helps manage classrooms, and supports early intervention through nudges, lessons, music, videos, activities, real time insights and evidence based strategies. Our goal is to build more peaceful, meaningful, and successful communities.

www.switch4schools.com.au

...and watch out for these warm fuzzies!

9 781923 746145